6 children's ministry essentials

A QUICK-ACCESS GUIDE

GPH®

Gospel Publishing House

6 children's ministry essentials

A QUICK-ACCESS GUIDE

GENERAL EDITOR, DICK GRUBER

contents

The Legacy I Want to Leave
Mark Entzminger

**Three Things I Wish I Had Known
When I Became a Kids Minister**
Jim Wideman

Looking Back
Randy Christensen

Early Lessons for a Children's Pastor
David Boyd

Three Tips for Effective Nursery Ministry
Mark Entzminger

Does Your Church Maintain a Welcoming, Fun, and Safe Nursery?
Cindy Grantham

The Church Nursery Is the Foundation for Discipleship
Mark Entzminger

Children's Ministry Is Not Childcare . . . or Is It?
Spencer Click

Don't Forget Preschool Kids
Mark Entzminger

Is Church for Boys?
Dan Metteer

Kids Ministry That Effectively Reaches Boys and Girls
Cara Railey

introduction

MY FIRST SUNDAY as a children's pastor, I moved my teaching materials and props into the local high school. Our congregation had outgrown the church building, so the children's church met in a high school music room. I had forty-some kids, no workers, and no training. God had saved and called me almost four years earlier. I took that four years of experience as a children's church helper/leader into that choir room and tried to have children's church. The first couple of years, our children's church teetered between deep prayer times and crazy games.

When I began my adventure in children's ministries back in the mid 1970s, there were few resources available for kids ministry leaders. The available materials were produced by Child Evangelism Fellowship, Sunday school curriculum publishing houses, and newly birthed KidMin supply houses, (Train Depot and One Way Street, now Creative Ministry Solutions, and Puppet Productions Inc.).

People who worked in kids ministry had no video resources, no worship music designed for children, and little training. Without cell phones or Internet, communication was limited to snail mail and long-distance phone calls. Networking with the handful of children's pastors across America was a challenge. Christian kid movies on 16mm film, filmstrips, flannel graph, and cassette players were considered cutting edge technology.

Thankfully times have changed!

What a privilege to serve in a day when so many resources for kids ministry are available. Curriculum abounds; media upgrades provide music, video support, and applications we only dreamed of in the past. The current market is flooded with books, training series on blue ray, blogs, digital magazines, and other E-materials. The challenge today is that with so much material, it takes a discerning children's leader to sort out the differences between mediocre and high-quality materials.

That's why I signed on to help compile this book. This collection of articles is written by some of the finest practitioners in children's ministry today. Each has a proven ministry and track record of providing training, help, and encouragement to those who serve children around the world. You'll find their insight understandable, valuable, and applicable.

Each chapter contains multiple articles that relate to a singular topic of discussion. These were made possible and available by the forward thinking Mark Entzminger. A couple of years ago, Mark established a KidMin blog with the idea to gather articles, produced by top writers in children's ministry, into a children's ministry training manual. Time has passed and the bloggers have written, under Mark's direction, on assigned topics. These were compiled for this book.

The contributors come from large and small churches. They hail from urban centers and rural settings. All have cut their teeth in the trenches of children's ministry. Each provides unique viewpoints, teaching, and inspiration for the children's leader of any sized community or church.

You'll discover a wealth of ministry-tested ideas. Some will be familiar and indicate you have been on the right track in your ministry. Others will challenge you to take a step of faith and witness growth you never dreamed possible. I have learned so much from each writer as I have poured through their writings to provide you with this collection of the best of the best. This isn't an all-inclusive book for the children's minister; it's a primer for the one who has served only a few months and a reminder for those who have served many years. I know you'll enjoy this work. God bless you in your ministry to His children.

—Dick Gruber, *General Editor*

the legacy
i want to leave

MARK ENTZMINGER

DO YOU EVER wonder what the person who replaces you in ministry will do differently? It's a scary and sobering thought at the same time. I have watched a number of ministry transitions take place over the years. Some of them have been successful; others have caused the ministry to flounder and never recover.

So what would I tell my successor I felt was important in shaping children's ministry? I thought you would never ask . . .

My approach to Bible teaching is intentional. The Bible is the core for any children's ministry. I think we all agree about that. But that's where the agreement tends to stop. It's important to me that kids understand the Bible as God's story. It's not a collection of stories of some dead people who lived a long time ago that can teach us good values and character traits. It's God's story of how He unveiled His plan to be in relationship with the crown of His creation—humankind—and how He longs to rescue people from their sins and their troubles. Each and every story teaches us something about the nature of God, which should impact our thoughts about Him and the life we live. By starting in Genesis and ending in Revelation, I want kids to see Yahweh as the thread that ties it all together. I want them to know that the story isn't complete; we are supporting actors just like Moses, Noah, and

Ruth. Please don't get caught up in the stories you want to tell; tell God's story.

Kids need to hear God's voice very clearly. In the family ministry movement a lot of emphasis is placed on the amount of hours a parent spends with their children each week. While this can't be dismissed, we also can't ignore that the Holy Spirit can speak to children any hour of the day—even when they're asleep. So how do we teach kids to recognize the voice of the Holy Spirit? Though there are a number of methods, none is more basic than helping them believe that when they read the Scripture they are hearing God's voice. Make sure you take time to read Scripture to the children in your ministry. Please don't fill every moment of the service with activity. Kids need an opportunity to listen to and respond to the Holy Spirit.

Boys and girls are different. By providing times to split into boys' and girls' groups, we do more than help manage the crowd. We maximize the way God wired us to learn and grow. There are some methods of discipleship that will work better in a group of girls than in a group of boys (and vice versa). Our goal is to create the best environment that will allow the next generation to see our faith and develop their personal faith. That means we don't just take into account what is age appropriate and what suits each child's preferred learning style, but we also understand that gender impacts our effectiveness as well. Boys need to see godly men; girls need to see godly women. Please don't give up on recruiting godly gender models who will be a living example of what you want your boys and girls to grow up to be.

Our focus on spiritually healthy marriages is the foundation of our family ministry model. Over the past decade "family ministry" has become a buzzword in the church world. And rightly so. For far too long the church had taken the responsibility of discipleship away from the parents—and the parents were far too agreeable about letting this happen. However, in all of the attempts to fix this, there is one approach that must not be overlooked: the importance of spiritually healthy marriages! Great spiritual parenting often results from a spiritually healthy marriage, but rarely does a spiritually healthy marriage grow from a focus on becoming a better parent. Please don't attempt to implement a family ministry model and assume that marriages will fix themselves. Make sure you have a strategy to save marriages before they start! Then paint pictures of what a spiritually healthy family can look like so they pursue that spiritual health for their family.

three things i wish i had known when i became a kids minister

JIM WIDEMAN

BACK IN 1977, when my pastor asked me to cover children's church for one Sunday, I had no idea that thirty-eight years later I would be writing to help other kids ministers. I also had no idea what God had in store for me. I'm thankful for all the wonderful doors, like this one, that He has opened. I'm also thankful for the early years I spent serving kids and families at Southside Assembly in Jackson, Mississippi. I'm still in contact with many of those kids. It's hard to believe that those first twelve-year-olds are turning fifty-one on their next birthday. (Thanks Facebook for making me feel old.)

I want to share with you three of the most important things I have learned through the years as a kids ministry leader:

1. *I must grow in my leadership skills.* A huge mistake I made in the early years was to focus on the kids who made up my ministry and forget to build a healthy ministry. I wish I had known how important it was to grow my leadership skills as well as my ministry. I understood that it was my job to help make healthy disciples. I understood the importance of training kids for a lifetime of service in a local church. But I didn't realize that a healthy leader must raise their own abilities to communicate and lead. It was years before I studied leadership books and worked to improve my abilities. When I wrote my first book, *Children's Ministry Leadership: The You-Can-Do-It Guide*, many children's pastors told me, "I wish I could have learned this from you twenty-five years ago." I always told them the same thing—I also wished I had known this stuff twenty-five years ago! The truth is, I had to choose to add leadership to my arsenal of puppets, costumes, and magic tricks.

2. *I must partner with parents.* The second thing I wish I had known is the importance of partnering with parents. You see, every teacher knows a child does better in school with help from their parents. This is also true with spiritual things. If I wanted to make healthy disciples, I needed to include parents. I wish I had known then what I know now: "What happens at home is more important than what happens at church."

3. *I must build a healthy ministry team.* The third thing I wish I had known is that you have to build a team, not only to build a healthy ministry but to make healthy disciples. In those early years, I was a one-man show. I now know that kids need other adults in their lives who will tell them the same thing their parents are saying at home. Besides that, you need a team to help you follow-up and care for kids. You can't do it alone. Building a team calls for duplication as well as delegation. Healthy disci-

pleship is a product of a healthy ministry built by a healthy team led by a healthy leader.

As you develop your leadership skills, partner with parents, and build a healthy team, your kids ministry will thrive and you will better relate to and win the respect and trust of your leadership.

looking back

RANDY CHRISTENSEN

THROUGH THE YEARS, I have served as a children's minister at churches with attendances of between 80 and 4,300 people. Though job descriptions changed from church to church, I found that most of the principles and ministry values remained the same. Here are three things I learned as a children's minister:

1. *Each person in the body of believers is important.* As children's ministers we argue that "People look at the outward appearance, but the LORD looks at the heart" (1 Samuel 16:7). The age of the person doesn't make an individual more important to God—whether young or old. We use that argument to prove the importance of ministry to kids. And, though that is true, I realize that just because a child is young, that doesn't make the child more important to God than someone who is older. I shouldn't allow the title of Kids Pastor to stop me from ministering to those in need. As a pastor, I should see people through the eyes of Jesus, and He is no respecter of persons—no matter their age.

I'm thankful for the opportunity to work with the younger saints for the majority of the time, but I have learned that a pastor ministers to every person in the body of Christ who has a need.

2. *I can choose to trust the wisdom and direction of my senior pastor.* Those in authority have a better view of "the big picture." In the body of Christ, I may be "the hand" reaching out to children, while my senior pastor is more like an eye or an ear. His role is to see and hear what God has for us as a whole body. He isn't against my vision for kids; he is *for* the whole body. We won't always agree, but I can choose to be agreeable. I can choose to trust my senior pastor.

Like a fitness trainer, he isn't just looking at the biceps. He's gauging what's best for the entire body, and I need to listen to him so the whole body can be healthy and strong.

3. *The best thing I can do is pray.* I rarely achieve all that I hope to accomplish in a day, but I have found that the best use of my time is the time I spend in prayer. When responsibilities overwhelm me, the best thing I can do is pray. When I'm planning future calendar events, I first pray. When preparing a kids sermon, rather than just jumping into a fun illustration, it's better if I just get alone somewhere and spend time in prayer. If I spend time in prayer, and become sensitive to God's voice, He will guide and direct my steps.

Instead of complaining about leadership decisions, it's better to pray for God to guide the decision makers.

I'm committed to living out these three crucial concepts. May the Lord guide and direct you too, my friends.

early lessons for a children's pastor

DAVID BOYD

THERE ARE THREE things I am particularly glad I learned early in my ministry with children.

1. Live by a set of principles. Early in ministry I was fortunate enough to learn the value of a code of ethics, or a set of standards to live by. I no longer remember who taught me this principle, but it has served me well. For me, three words became a guide to live by—a prayer to keep me focused. The prayer was, "Lord keep me *holy, humble*, and *anointed.*"

Each of these terms can make or break your ministry: Without holiness your ministry will fail; without humility your ministry will eventually be frustrated and your marriage will struggle; without anointing your ministry will be a fraction of what God intended it to be. Choose a set of principles to live by. Ask God to guide you on your journey and be the best you can be.

2. Quality people equal quality ministry. Yet quality people are tough to find. They seem unwilling to become a part of children's ministry. This could be due to busy lifestyles or because they have been burned out in the past. Building a team of quality people can be a daunting task. So how does it happen? I believe the basis of building a successful long-term team centers on the ability to love and care for people. Open your home to families in the church. Care for the leaders you have. Reach new families who can eventually become part of your team. Ultimately, building a team begins with opening your life up to people. It takes time, it takes patience, and it takes hard work.

3. Help kids learn to hear God's voice. I have served as a children's leader long enough to have seen huge numbers of kids grow and thrive in their relationship with the Lord. Many are now pastors and missionaries. What makes a child's spiritual roots grow deep? There are many factors, but let me mention just one—the ability to hear God's voice. This happens through prayer and worship. Often it happens at the altar.

The altar is often missing in today's kids church. Services are tightly scheduled to entertain and hold kids' attention. The thought of giving kids ten to fifteen minutes to seek God seems like an unplanned event. Yet at kids camps I have seen kids pray for over an hour! What's the difference? At kids camp we plan for kids to seek God, search for Him, hear from Him, and talk to Him. Kids who learn to hear God's voice early are more likely to receive His instructions, choose to obey Him, and become His followers for life.

CHAPTER 1
nursery and preschool

IN 2005, I joined with a team to plant a church in my community in Pennsylvania. In an effort to insure that our nursery was established with high standards, I visited several local church plants. Each was meeting in a school, as we would be, and each had developed their version of a portable nursery. I observed friendly people in every case and in two out of three, poor security, badly used furnishings, and garage sale toys. I would not have trusted those nurseries with my grandchildren.

Kathy and Don were new parents. They attended our church just a little bit longer than their four-month old newborn had been on planet earth. They toured our nursery to insure that it would be a pleasant, safe environment for their precious firstborn daughter. After experiencing our nursery, one of them shared, "We love the nursery. It's so clean and the people are so friendly that we will definitely trust them with our daughter."

Parents like this place a trust in the church nursery and its workers. Before they can relax in church and enjoy a baby-free Sunday morning, they must be assured that the nursery staff will care for their child in a safe, clean, and positive environment.

My friend Sandy Askew used to tell me that evangelism in a child's life begins in the nursery. The nursery and then preschool are places where a child first develops a love for God's Word and feelings about family, the church, and the gospel. This is where loving workers begin to reinforce a growing pre-evangelism vocabulary. Then, when children are old enough, they have the tools to make that first commitment to Christ.

I remember a dad named Jason in one church. He served in the three-year-old classroom. Jason sat on the floor and played guitar while children danced and sang all around him. One dad volunteered to work in the class because of what he saw when Jason ministered to those precious children.

Our nurseries and preschool rooms need teams of loving, joyful, well-trained servants. The men and women in these rooms must be the best and brightest. First impressions made in these crucial years will determine the future and eternity for these children. Just as much care, prayer, and planning is necessary to oversee these areas as the children's church and clubs. —D. G.

Three Tips for Effective Nursery Ministry
MARK ENTZMINGER

When it comes to nursery ministry, most church leaders focus on creating a safe environment where parents feel comfortable leaving their children during church. However, the importance of the nursery ministry goes well beyond creating a safe environment. In fact, I believe it's the best place to establish a foundation for spiritual growth for kids.

There's no denying that the first three years of a child's life are the most critical time period for personal development. Between conception and age three, a child's brain undergoes an impressive amount of change. At birth, it already has almost all of the neurons it will ever have. It doubles in size in the first year, and by age three it has reached 80 percent of its adult volume.[1]

Here are three things you can do to maximize your opportunity to establish a foundation for spiritual growth in your nursery ministry.

1. *Be intentional with visual stimulation*: The remarkable visual abilities of newborn babies highlight how rapid prenatal brain development occurs. Newborns can recognize human faces, which they prefer over other objects, and can even discriminate between happy and sad expressions.

How can you be more intentional with visual stimulation in your nursery? Remind nursery volunteers to smile and make eye contact with babies and toddlers throughout the time they are in your care. Look for ways to incorporate visual activities in your lessons with toddlers.

2. *Incorporate audio learning*: There's not a lot of audio interaction with babies in most nursery environments. However, intentionally communicating with babies could be one of the most valuable things your volunteers do each Sunday.

Babies experience a lot of sensations, especially hearing. According to one study, during their first year of life babies can already respond to language preferences including the difference between the language spoken by the parent and a foreign language, the voice of the mother and a stranger, and words of significance and insignificance.[2]

What does this mean for your nursery ministry? Be sure to incorporate audio learning with the babies in your care. Tell Bible stories. Pray blessings over the child. Sing worship songs or play worship music.

3. *Create consistency*: The nursery is often the area of ministry with the least consistency when it comes to volunteers and the Sunday morning experience. While you might not be able to change your approach to nursery ministry overnight, there are some things you can do to create a consistent environment for

kids. Be consistent in the songs you sing and stories you tell. Adequately train volunteers about the importance of stimulating babies and toddlers with God-filled interactions. This will increase the likelihood that these behaviors and emotional responses will be imprinted on their minds. What can you do today? Ensure every worker understands the importance of their role.

http://kids.healthychurch.com/healthy-ministry/three-tips-for-effective-nursery-ministry

Does Your Church Maintain a Welcoming, Fun, and Safe Nursery?

CINDY GRANTHAM

A nursery can be a raucous place! The crash of toys, little babbling voices, and even crying are heard at various times— even all at the same time. How can you and your nursery staff instill confidence in your church families and visitors so they feel comfortable and confident in leaving their precious little ones in your care? Paying attention to the following areas will leave nothing but the most positive impression.

1. *Make your nursery attractive*: Decor that is visually engaging and geared specifically for babies and toddlers lends professionalism to a nursery space. Make sure there are no safety issues such as open electrical outlets or cords hanging from blinds. Use bright but tasteful colors on walls, floors, furnishings, and equipment. Add fun toys and your nursery will make children feel welcome and will engage parents in your ministry.

2. *Keep it clean*: Pay detailed attention to safe sanitation procedures for the room's surfaces and the toys. Ensure that the space is always clean and smells fresh. No one wants to leave their little one in a room that reeks with foul odors or harsh chemical smells.

3. *Staff it well*: Schedule adequate staff who are well trained. Every children's minister should be aware of the state guidelines that determine your adult-to-child ratios in a childcare setting. Additionally, the staff should be properly trained on check-in procedures, parent contact guidelines, and basic first aid. Don't forget to coach your staff how to greet parents and children. Consider that the nursery workers could be the first church members a visitor will meet. Remind the nursery staff to be friendly, confident, and to ask questions. Parents will feel more at ease when they interact with nursery volunteers who take time to be thorough and learn about the needs of each child.

4. *Create a safe check-in system*: A check-in system that garners confidence is a *must*. Many larger churches have elaborate electronic arrangements, but few smaller churches can afford a high-tech system. If that is the case in your church, you must still have a process in place that makes parents and nursery volunteers feel comfortable and protected. This should include name tags for the child and their possessions, information cards with a parent's contact details, and a list of allergies and other vital data. Make sure your volunteers are able to contact parents during the service if needed. Lastly, don't forget to have a safe system in place to match parents and children for pick up.

5. *Pray over it*: The most important thing children's pastors can do for their weekly ministries is to pray. So many times we get bogged down in the business of preparing and doing that we neglect our divine appointment. The impact of surrounding your volunteers, church families, and visitors in prayer will impact both the concrete and spiritual worlds.

These are a few of the essential points for creating a nursery that puts parents at ease and offers a safe and fun environment for children. The week-to-week implementation is not difficult once the nursery staff is comfortable with the weekly procedures. Any amount of time spent creating a plan and training the workers will reap multiple benefits in the long run when parents and visitors sense the care, love, and prayer you have put into your nursery plan.

http://kids.healthychurch.com/healthy-ministry/your-nursery-impression

The Church Nursery Is the Foundation for Discipleship
MARK ENTZMINGER

When I talk with ministry leaders about the idea of cradle-to-grave discipleship, many assume I'm highlighting the importance of kids ministry in general. But is it possible that your church's nursery is the most important place for spiritual growth?

Unfortunately, many churches see the nursery as a glorified babysitting service. Because we don't see the tangible results of our efforts like we do in ministry to older kids, we can quickly start to believe the myth that the nursery doesn't matter as long as babies are changed and happy when their caregiver arrives to pick them up.

Granted, newborns sleep most of the day, they can't use language, and their motor skills aren't honed. But this doesn't mean they aren't learning and growing. Could it be that the first few months and years of a baby's life are the most significant for planting and watering the seeds of faith in that little heart?

Jeremiah 1:5 reminds us that God knew Jeremiah before he was born. "Before I formed you in the womb, I knew you." We forget that a newborn baby already has nine months of life experience prior to birth. But Scripture isn't the only place that talks about the importance of your nursery. Do a quick Google search and you'll find thousands of articles that discuss how important the first three years of a child's life are for spiritual development.

Could it be that we have underestimated the spiritual impact of nursery ministry?

How can you establish a foundation for spiritual growth in your nursery? Here are three keys to help you.

1. *Don't ignore the baby when you greet the parents each week.* Because babies won't smile right away or tell you what's going on in their lives, it's easy for volunteers to focus their attention on the parent or caregiver who leaves the baby at the nursery. However, interacting with the baby or toddler right away is important.

Whenever babies and toddlers are being dropped off, encourage your volunteers to make eye contact, greet the baby or toddler by name, and utilize appropriate physical touch.

2. *Remember to engage with audio and visual elements.* Babies' minds are growing at the fastest rate they'll ever experience. Their ears, eyes, movement, and touch are all taking in signals that are being imprinted on their brains.

Author T. Berry Brazelton explains that reading to children, responding to their smiles with a smile, returning their vocalizations with one of your own, touching them, holding them—all of these further a child's brain development and future potential, even in the earliest months.[3] Rather than sitting in a comfortable chair and holding a baby and talking with other workers, encourage your nursery staff to read stories or sing songs to the baby. Use the name of the baby and make eye contact with the baby. Talk about the wonderful way God has made him or her.

3. *Teach the importance of your nursery.* There are hundreds of resources when it comes to maximizing the first three years of a child's life. This is a critical time of development in the life of a baby or toddler. Your children's leaders and nursery workers should all take time to learn and understand the minds of children. Develop a resource that teaches nursery volunteers about

the valuable role they play and train them to proactively interact with babies in a way that will enhance spiritual growth.

http://kids.healthychurch.com/healthy-kids/how-important-is-the-church-nursery

Children's Ministry Is Not Childcare . . . or Is It?
SPENCER CLICK

One of the great mantras of children's ministry is that we aren't childcare. But I think we need to reconsider that idea because part of our job in ministry *is* childcare.

Creating a safe and secure environment for the children in our churches is a vital element of this ministry—we need to treat the safety of the children entrusted to us with the same level of seriousness as local preschools, day care centers, and Chuck-E-Cheese! (These are all non-ministry locations that take child security seriously!) When we think in terms of childcare, safety, and security, we don't belittle the ministry—we enhance it!

Frame it this way—you may have the most spectacular ministry on the planet, but if you lose or maim a child due to carelessness or negligence, your ministry won't matter. Parents won't trust you regardless of how well you teach the gospel.

So, what policies and procedures do you have in place to ensure that the kids in your church are safe and secure while they learn about Jesus and have fun?

Here are some things we have in place to help parents feel at ease with the quality of care their children will receive when they come to our church:

- Every child has a unique security tag, and only an adult with the corresponding tag can pick up the child. We also have a "lost tag" process in place.

This is bothersome, so most parents only lose their tag once.

- Two adults are always in the room with the kids. Married adults count as one adult.

- Adults don't use kids' bathrooms and vice versa.

- We maintain hallway roamers: men from our risk management team walk the hallways to ensure that no one is in the children's area who shouldn't be.

- We have eliminated all hiding spots. All our classrooms have windows in the doors, and places that can be "out-of-sight" are locked to eliminate opportunities to hide.

- Safety is everyone's job.

- "Why are you here?" We train our front-desk volunteers, teachers, and hallway roamers to ask this question all the time (although politely) to folks who look out of place. They know we're there for the kids and protecting them is part of that job!

Why is this all so important? Because we live in an unsafe world. Late last year, a church in our area failed to follow the procedures recommended above and the unthinkable happened. A parent who was in a custody fight came to church and picked up the kids; now they're gone ... due to negligence and failure of a church to ensure the safety of those kids.

Parents won't entrust their children to the childcare staff of your church unless they feel their children are safe. If they don't feel safe to leave their children, you won't have the opportunity to minister to the children or to their parents. Take safety and security seriously—it is childcare that makes a world of difference in your effectiveness in ministry!

http://kids.healthychurch.com/healthy-leaders/childrens-ministry-is-not-childcare

Don't Forget Preschool Kids
MARK ENTZMINGER

In the kid ministry world it's common for churches to focus most of their time and energy on the elementary-age group. There are typically more curriculum options available for that group, and many consider it more "fun" to work with them because of their physical and mental development. But don't forget about preschoolers.

Here are three benefits of being intentional with preschoolers in your church:

1. *Easier transition*: When the elementary team is conscientious about connecting with preschool children before they transition up, they'll likely have a relational foundation to start from. This can make all the difference in helping these young kids feel like they have a friend who knows them and cares about them.

2. *First, lasting impressions*: The good or bad experiences of preschool will likely stick with the child for many years. Though some of the children may have grown up in the church from the nursery, most won't have any memories of church until they're in preschool. As we minister intentionally, with the "end in mind," we must think about the first, lasting impressions a child will have. Intentionality with preschoolers can help them fall in love with God's house and God's people.

3. *Intentionality demonstrates excellence to parents*: Preschool intentionality means lessons are age appropriate, teachers are trained for that specific age group, and class rooms are clean and equipped

with plenty of age-appropriate activities and games. When this happens, young parents will see and appreciate the level of excellence your church takes with even the smallest members of the congregation.

Preschool children may or may not be your "sweet spot" of ministry. However, with some intentionality and partnering with people who are passionate experts in this age group, you can set your children's ministry on a trajectory of positive impact.

http://kids.healthychurch.com/healthy-kids/dont-forget-preschool-kids

CHAPTER 2
gender-specific children's ministry

THERESA WAS TWELVE when her parents brought her to our church. After two Sundays, she didn't feel welcome. Her mom talked with me about this, and I recommended they come on Wednesday night so their daughter could attend our girls' club program. That is where Theresa made friends, became comfortable with our style of worship, and learned that church can be fun. Her friends from Wednesday night helped her adjust to children's worship on Sunday mornings. What could have been a lost opportunity of ministry turned into a testimony because of a gender-sensitive ministry.

I walked down a hall on a Wednesday night and spied two Ranger boys and a commander sitting on the floor outside the door to their class. As I approached, it became evident that one boy was leading the other boy to Christ, with the encouragement of his commander. The boy knew just what to say to his friend as he led him into a time of prayer. I remember thinking that the soil of the new Christian's heart had been prepared in a room full of boys, acting like boys and doing guy things. I was blessed.

Since my early days as a children's pastor, I have seen incredible ministry in the children's church. Boys and girls have worshiped side by side, prayed at altars, and even taught lessons.

I have also witnessed the blessing of gender-specific ministries. Club ministries, Royal Rangers, and MPact Girls provide a fun environment for boys and girls to express themselves freely among their own gender. Leaders are free to disciple boys and girls in gender-specific ways that would never appeal to the other.

Here's a news flash: Boys and girls are different! God created them that way, male and female. The differences only begin with the physical/biological uniqueness. Emotions, thought processes, and cultural interests are distinct. Boys need godly men to serve as mentors and models. Girls need the influence of godly women who find their significance and self-respect in a relationship with Christ.

I know that you'll be inspired to ramp up your club ministries after reading this chapter. See what our writers have to say about the value of gender-specific ministries in the overall picture of ministry to children and families. —D. G.

Is Church for Boys?
DAN METTEER

As I have watched my son grow up, I have noticed that he picks up very quickly which things are "boy" things: skateboards, Legos®, superheroes, Star Wars—these things are second nature to him. Not only does he notice these things, he's obsessed with them.

As he continues to grow, I notice how he continually watches what the older boys around him do—how they talk, what they do, even how they move—and he tries to emulate them. At home, he watches me. He notices what I do, what I wear, and he tries to copy me. He often talks about what he will be like when he is a dad. I guess this is the way we grow up.

But there's a problem with the way boys are growing up today. They are resisting going to church. According to a recent survey of churches in the U.S., church attendance is 61 percent female and only 39 percent male.[4] There are probably several reasons for this imbalance, but one reason is undeniable: When you walk up and down the hallways of your children's ministries, look in the classrooms. Who are the leaders? By far, the majority of children's ministries volunteers are women.

Most churches are painfully lacking in fathers, grandfathers, and older brothers who want to serve kids at church. And this lack of visible male presence around kids in our church sends kids a silent but disastrous message week after week: Church isn't a place for men. As boys form their identities, they need role models. If we hope to keep boys in the church when they become men, our children's ministries must have men to mentor young boys.

This isn't to belittle the female volunteers who work among our children, but to call men to help in this ministry. We need men to show the next generation that the church is worth their time—that it's more important than career, hobbies, and work around the house. We need men who will be willing examples of obedience to Jesus' mandate to value children.

If every man in the church gave one hour per month to serve kids at church, the church would look radically different in twenty years. So let's do it! My sons and grandsons thank you in advance.
http://kids.healthychurch.com/healthy-kids/is-church-for-boys

Kids Ministry That Effectively Reaches Boys and Girls
CARA RAILEY

If we want to create an environment where each boy and girl in our ministry has the best opportunity to grow as a Spirit-filled disciple of Christ, we must value gender-specific mentoring and discipleship.

There are many reasons why gender-specific discipleship is an important aspect of kids ministry. One of the most basic is that girls and boys learn differently. For optimal learning and discipleship to occur, each gender needs the methods that work best for them. Another reason is that we need to address different topics for girls and for boys. Gender-specific mentoring allows you to guide kids in your ministry through separate topics and mentorship opportunities.

Let me share some insights for creating gender-specific discipleship opportunities in your ministry that will help kids grow as healthy disciples. Here are six components that will maximize the opportunity of gender-specific discipleship:

1. *Provide discipleship and leadership training for leaders and volunteers.* There's no way you can disciple each individual child in your ministry. Your Sunday school teachers or small-group leaders are on the front lines of helping kids grow. As kids ministry leaders, one of the best things we can do is focus on training leaders to disciple kids rather than simply focusing on how to run a program or use a curriculum. Training and equipping leaders in the areas of role modeling, accountability, bonding, and leading kids through a discipleship process is essential for creating a healthy kids ministry where kids will truly grow.

2. *Create small-group environments where discipleship can thrive.* Breaking larger groups of kids down into groups of five to eight is the best way to ensure each kid has the opportunity to be discipled by a mentor who truly knows them. This also allows your small-group leaders to create unique environments based on the kids in their group.

3. *Make sure your content and curriculum is current and relevant for boys and girls in your ministry.* It's important that your leaders are aware of the current issues boys and girls face and are trained

to provide godly counsel that addresses those issues. Relevant content and engaging teaching methods are critically important, especially for boys who can become easily distracted or bored.

4. *Host gender-specific ministry outreach events as a way to create momentum.* While boys and girls in youth ministry might share the same interests, boys and girls in kids ministry share vastly different interests. That's why I encourage leaders to look for unique ways to create gender-specific outreach events that are geared specifically towards boys or girls. Hosting events that allow each gender to invite their friends is a great way to build momentum throughout the year.

5. *Build a system where numerous stakeholders have vested interest in your gender-specific ministry opportunities.* In addition to encouraging parents to buy into the opportunity, look for staff members or key volunteers in your church who understand the value in gender-specific discipleship and ask for their help. One important part of building a system of stakeholders is to look for people who can help shape your ministry. Don't just view stakeholders as people who supply money or resources, but look for people who can help shape the direction of your ministry by investing their time and energy.

6. *Take a holistic approach to discipleship for both boys and girls.* One of the things we believe at My Healthy Church is that a healthy disciple is one who is growing in every area of life: spiritually, relationally, intellectually, emotionally, and physically. As you evaluate your gender-specific discipleship strategies, make sure to evaluate each one based on those five criteria. You might find that your strategy for boys is struggling in an area that your girls' ministry is not. Evaluating each separately allows you to ensure that both boys and girls are becoming healthy, Spirit-filled disciples.

http://kids.healthychurch.com/healthy-ministry/kidmin-that-effectively-reaches-boys-and-girls

Three Reasons Why Kids Thrive in Gender-Specific Ministry
JOSH DRYER

If you were to do a quick Google search for "Kids Ministry Model," you would be flooded with hundreds of ideas! There are all kinds of models for kids ministry in the local church. For instance you would find large group, small group, video-driven, gender-specific ministries, and family focus just to name a few. The curriculum options are endless, with all sorts of philosophies. I have found the gender-specific ministry model to be successful because it enhances kids' learning.

Here are three reasons I find why kids thrive in gender-specific ministries:

1. *A rich environment*: Growing up in Oklahoma City, each spring meant tornado season—April through June! As kids, many afternoons were spent glued to the TV as the meteorologists and storm chasers gave us play-by-play coverage of where the storms were and whether or not a tornado was coming! They often talked about how the "environment" and "atmosphere" were providing the perfect conditions for a tornado to form. Moisture from the Gulf of Mexico, and colliding high and low pressures systems were usually the key ingredients.

In a similar manner, gender-specific ministries can create rich environments for spiritual growth to take place in boys and girls! Boys and girls learn differently: Boys learn through action, repetition, and topics that grab their attention. Girls love to collaborate with other girls, like tidy spaces, and meticulously work through projects. Gender-specific ministries also allow for more comfortable environments for boys and girls to share about gender-specific issues and challenges. Creating an environment that best allows boys and girls to learn based on their gender traits allows for more effective discipleship!

2. *Biblical mentoring:* One of the best examples of mentoring is found in Scripture. Paul and Timothy provide the perfect illustration of how a mentor can speak life into a young person's life! We don't know everything about Timothy's early life, but we do know his mother was Jewish and his father was Greek. We may easily fly over this when we're reading, but for the culture of the day, this was a big no-no! Half-Jewish people were often hated by the Jewish people of that day, and Timothy's mother may have been a social outcast. Some commentators believe Timothy grew up in a broken home with either a deadbeat dad and/or just a single mom. Timothy's mother may have prayed that a godly man would mentor her son, and she got the very best in Paul! Gender-specific ministries harness the power of men and women mentoring rather than teaching. Mentoring flows out of life experiences and knowledge and is enhanced because of relationship. Teachers impart knowledge; mentors impart life and spiritual growth. The trust and wisdom that mentoring relationships impart into a child's life are things a curriculum can't buy.

3. *Fostering friendships:* I once heard a story of a bird owner who wanted his parrots to sing like his parakeet. So he put his parakeet in the cage with his parrots and left them for a week. When he returned, he was shocked to learn that instead of his parrots singing beautifully like the parakeet, his parakeet was talking like the parrots! This happened because there were many parrots to influence the parakeet but only one parakeet to influence the parrots. This story shows the importance of the people around our children. It's vital to foster godly friendships that will encourage kids to live Spirit-empowered lives! Gender-specific ministries create environments for kids to build and develop friendships with other boys and girls who are running after God!

These friends will become a circle of influence that will have a positive rather than a destructive influence.

Consider how you can use gender-specific ministry in your church to provide opportunities for kids to thrive and chase after God.

http://kids.healthychurch.com/healthy-ministry/three-reasons-kids-thrive-in-gender-specific-ministry

How to Add Gender-Specific Opportunities to Your Kids Ministry

SCOTT BERKEY

What comes to mind when you hear someone say "gender-specific ministry"? It can be, and in many ways has become, a buzzword in the world of children's ministry. There are certainly incredible tools for ministering to boys, and I have seen just as many (if not more) great curriculums for teaching girls. If we aren't careful though, it can get complicated pretty quickly. Remember this simple truth: You have both boys and girls in your ministry and it's your responsibility to minister to both groups. Here are three ways to creatively add gender-specific activities to your children's ministry environments:

1. *Small groups:* Simply adding a ten to fifteen minute small-group element to your weekend kids church service will allow ministry to happen to boys and girls in more unique ways. We have found that separating kids by age and gender allows them to open up more and discuss freely what they have learned. They're more comfortable with their peers and experience less anxiety compared to when they're around members of the opposite sex.

2. *Special events:* If your calendar is anything like mine, it's probably completely full. When was the last time you evaluated what you were doing in the light of gender-specific ministries?

It's great to have attractive events, but rather than just having another fun time, why not be intentional? Develop an activity with a specific gender in mind. Hosting a "knights and princesses" event will allow your team to talk to boys and girls separately about what it means to be a man or a woman of God (adding dress-up elements to this idea will certainly make it a picture-worthy affair).

3. *Discipleship classes*: If your church has a midweek service, you have a natural opportunity to insert gender-specific classes. Something special happens when a group of girls or boys come together for class (this might include giggling for the girls and horsing around for the boys). Even if you choose the same curriculum for both groups, your teachers will naturally teach differently if only one gender is present in the room.

Gender-specific ministry doesn't have to be complicated. Take what you're already doing and look at it through the lens of the gender-specific needs of boys and girls. Sometimes simply giving them unique opportunities to learn exclusively with their same gender will go a long way in making the ministry you lead a healthy kids ministry!

http://kids.healthychurch.com/healthy-kids/why-gender-specific-ministry

Capturing the Hearts of Boys and Girls
CARA RAILEY

Gender-specific mentoring can be a critical component in any healthy discipling relationship. While I wholeheartedly believe we can be discipled by the opposite gender, I also believe that if you're a man, it's important to learn from other men (and vice-versa). The importance of gender-specific ministry is greatest in the area of children's ministry. If we truly want to capture the hearts of boys and girls, we must understand their God-given uniqueness.

In developing gender-specific ministry programs for our denomination (Mpact for girls and Royal Rangers for boys), we have learned some significant things in our research:

1. *Gender-specific discipleship solves the challenges of finding positive role models for kids in your ministry.* There has been a lot of conversation about the lack of positive role models for many of today's young boys. Gender-specific discipleship allows your kids ministry to help fill that void. At the same time, providing female leaders for girls in your ministry is an essential way to show them they can play a valuable role in ministry when most church staffs are made up of men.

2. *Gender-specific discipleship helps eliminate distractions.* Maybe it's the result of gender-based competition, flirting, sexual tension, or a combination of all of these, but the hard fact is that separating boys and girls results in increased focus and concentration.

3. *Gender-specific discipleship allows girls and boys to be more open in discussing personal issues.* In most cases, boys and girls struggle with different issues. For example, many girls struggle with self-image or self-value while boys struggle with topics related to authority or maturing into a godly man. The sooner we put girls and boys in a safe environment to talk about these challenging subjects, the sooner these issues can be handled successfully.

4. *Gender-specific discipleship naturally creates stronger bonds.* The bonds forged through mentoring give girls a listening ear and give boys camaraderie.

It goes without saying that we need to minister to boys and girls together, but some of the most effective discipleship occurs when genders are separated. Don't miss the opportunity to reach your kids in this specific way.

http://kids.healthychurch.com/healthy-ministry/capturing-the-hearts-of-boys-and-girls

Summary Activities for Boys

BRAD SHIMOMURA

Are you familiar with the summer drop-off in church attendance? You know the drill: school lets out and families take trips. Camping, fishing, and other family events seem to take precedence over church for a couple of months. I know it all too well. But rather than dread the summer months, I like to think that summer activities are a great way to keep connected with our church kids at a time when we might not see them in weekend services.

Psychologists have found that while girls connect more with face-to-face contact, boys connect more when they do things together. Many men will tell you that their best memories with their fathers or other adult male role models took place while they were fishing, working on cars, or doing other fun activities together. With that in mind, here are some ideas of how to connect with boys during the summer drop-off.

1. *MEGA Sports Camp is a great place to start!* Think: VBS meets sports clinics. Each day, the kids come and learn skills to improve in their sport, and they get to hear a gospel message. MEGA Sports Camp is highly customizable and doesn't actually require expert coaches. The material is laid out so that almost anyone with a rudimentary knowledge of the sport, a heart for kids, and a fun-loving spirit can help. Even someone with zero sports experience can participate by helping with things like snacks, nursing, setup, music, teaching, and many others. With MEGA Sports Camp you can choose to teach any combination of soccer, flag football, basketball, baseball, and cheerleading.

2. *A carless drive-in movie is a great way to engage boys.* You can use your parking lot, playground, or a local park (check with your local parks and recreation department for permits and

reservation information). Invite kids and families to watch a movie on a big screen outdoors. Use a movie that has some redemptive value and can be used to start a conversation about God. After the movie is over, have a discussion about what lessons can be learned and how they apply to life. For extra fun, invite kids to make a car out of boxes or other disposable material, and give a prize for the best car design. Anytime you show a movie or movie clip, make sure you have the proper licensing to do so. CVLI, which is similar to CCLI, has some options for obtaining the license. Also, remember to preview the movie ahead of time. A movie you have seen 100 times still looks different when you think about showing it as a church event to children.

3. *For a low-key event, consider having an outdoor adventure day for boys.* For example, have a fishing day. Tell your church kids to invite their friends who don't go to church, and spend the day on the water fishing, swimming, and having fun. Take a few minutes to share a Bible story that involves fishing and share the gospel. Be sure to check your local municipalities for fishing license requirements or other park use information. You might also consider a hiking trip, river rafting, or an outdoor scavenger hunt.

Summer events come in all shapes and sizes, from the more organized like VBS, to something as simple as a fishing trip and a conversation about God, and everything in-between. Doing summer events can sound like a big deal when you think only about big events like VBS. The most important thing is to do something to stay connected with your boys during the summer months.

http://kids.healthychurch.com/healthy-ministry/summer-activities-for-boys

Summer Activities for Girls

HEATHER MARBLE

"Bees'll buzz, kids'll blow dandelion fuzz." I promise I won't sing the entire song "Summer" from the movie Frozen, but summer is one of my most favorite seasons! Growing up I remember days spent on the lake, times with my family, barbecues, swimming in the pool, and going for walks. Summer is a *blast* and such a key time for families to get outside and spend quality time together! Something other than being stuck inside watching Frozen one more time, summer gives kids a chance to explore and build relationships with other kids their age. Here are a few things that I loved about summer and some ideas for you to share with your daughters:

1. *Pedicures for flip-flops:* This is one summer "must-do" with your daughter. During a mother/daughter date, stop and get pedicures. Not only are they relaxing, but your toes will look adorable in flip-flops.

2. *Chalk creations:* One of the coolest ideas I have experienced is allowing kids to draw with chalk on a trampoline, if you have one. It's so much fun, and the first rain will wash it off. Other ideas include jumping hopscotch or seeing who can jump the furthest.

3. *Swimming and pool parties:* Pools are an amazing way not only to cool down but to build relationships with neighborhood kids. Invite the school friends that your kids might be missing during summer. Cook some hot dogs or hamburgers and have everyone bring a dish to share. Enjoy the time of fellowship and playing some of your favorite pool games: Marco Polo, Cannonballs, Handstands, etc. Summer is the perfect time to splish and splash.

4. *Squirt-gun painting:* One of my favorite ideas is to pin long sheets of paper to your outdoor clothesline. Then have your girls

take squirt guns filled with kid-friendly paint mixed with water and shoot it at the paper. It makes such fun art projects while being outside. Another painting craft is mixing food coloring with bubbles and then blowing them against the paper and seeing the splattered marks turn into art!

5. *Backyard movie nights and bonfires*: One of my friends bought a cheap projector, and after the sun goes down he puts a movie in to watch on the side of his house. It's one of the coolest experiences! Partner that with a small bonfire, and you have a perfect evening under the stars. (If you have never had a s'more with a peanut-butter cup, do so; it will change your life.)

6. *Family hikes/walks*: Another fun thing to do with your daughters over the summer is to spend time outside hiking or going for an evening walk. It's the perfect time to stay active and enjoy the warmth!

Summer is the time to explore, create, and build memories that last. Spending time together is one of those things that will make your daughter's summer even brighter!

http://kids.healthychurch.com/healthy-kids/summer-activities-for-girls

CHAPTER 3
spirit-empowered children's ministry

HE WASN'T AFRAID of the dark. At eight years old, Tom was afraid of his dreams. Each night he prayed with his parents and drifted to sleep listening to Christian music. His parents hung Scriptures on his walls and didn't let him watch television after dinner. None of this helped. Tom still had night terrors. His dreams were so intensely scary that he couldn't wake from them. His father would sit on the edge of the bed as Tom cried for help. Together they repeated Bible verses. Eventually, the dream would cease and Tom would lie down to sleep through the rest of the night. Nothing changed for nearly a year. Then Tom was baptized in the Holy Spirit. The next time he had a bad dream, Tom's father encouraged him to pray in his prayer language. Tom did, the dream ended, and he never had another night terror.

More than ever before, children need the power and presence of God in their lives. Sin abounds in this world. When children receive the baptism in the Holy Spirit, they become empowered to pray with more effectiveness, to overcome temptation, to understand God's Word in a deeper way, and to witness to their friends.

Pentecost and the Holy Spirit baptism are an essential part of a balanced children's program. It isn't enough to send kids to camp once a year for their annual dose of Full Gospel teaching. Your children's ministry must be a place that welcomes the Holy Spirit, embraces Pentecost, and regularly provides answers to children's questions about the Pentecostal experience.

But how do we present Pentecost, the baptism in the Holy Spirit, and Holy Spirit power to children? Some of my favorite writers have addressed these and more questions in the following pages. Read this and study the move of the Spirit in the early church. Don't shy away from this important aspect of children's ministry. If you haven't yet received this second wonderful gift, meditate on what is written and pray for more of Jesus. There's no greater joy than to experience the power of God through the worship, preaching, and prayer times in your children's church.

I know that armed with Scripture, the teachings in this chapter, and a determination to experience the fullness of Christ, you'll enjoy His presence in your children's ministry in deeper ways than you thought possible. Trust God and seek His face. Give the children of your church the opportunity to experience the mighty power of the Holy Spirit. —D. G.

Kids and Spirit Empowerment
MARK ENTZMINGER

I'm concerned about this generation of children having a genuine Pentecostal experience and understanding. I'm concerned because I have heard far too many leaders share misconceptions about what it means to be Pentecostal. These misconceptions are creeping into the things we teach our children about the baptism in the Holy Spirit.

Let me share some key perspectives that must shape how we teach children about the baptism in the Holy Spirit.

Jesus is the Baptizer. For some, this may sound like an unnecessary clarification. But in fact it's very important. John the Baptist introduced Jesus as "after me comes one who is more powerful than I. . . . He will baptize you with the Holy Spirit and fire." (Matthew 3:11). Jesus is the Baptizer; He is the One who gives the gift of the Holy Spirit.

All believers have the Holy Spirit. I have heard many people indicate that if someone is not baptized in the Holy Spirit they are missing out on the work of the Holy Spirit in their lives. The truth of the matter is that the Holy Spirit is at work even in the life of an unbeliever. In this case, the Spirit draws them to the Father. The Holy Spirit's work is not limited to those who have been baptized in the Spirit and speak in tongues. However, the Scripture is very clear that the initial physical evidence of the baptism in the Holy Spirit is speaking in an unlearned language (Acts 2:4; 10:46; 19:6).

The Holy Spirit didn't arrive in Acts 2. The Holy Spirit was active in creation and throughout human history as recorded in the Old Testament. The supervising craftsmen who worked on the tabernacle (Bezalel and Oholiab), Samson, Saul, David, Elijah, and Elisha are just a few who acted under the power of the Holy Spirit. If we don't provide children with an accurate understanding of the role of the Holy Spirit they will misunderstand His working in the world today.

However, Acts 2 did mark the beginning of a new era in the outpouring of the Holy Spirit on all believers. In the Old Testament, the Holy Spirit acted through a select number of people. The Day of Pentecost marked the beginning of a time when the Holy Spirit became available to be poured out "on all people," (Acts 2:17) not just those selected as prophets, judges, priests, or kings.

Being Pentecostal is more than a belief. Let's stop talking about the baptism in the Holy Spirit as something we believe in. Let's bring the power of the Holy Spirit into our everyday lives. Do kids know they can receive a word of knowledge from the Holy Spirit while they're sitting at their school desks? Have they ever been impressed to pray for healing during a soccer game? Is the fruit of the Spirit growing in their lives?

We must live and teach about the Holy Spirit in a way that reveals His power to the next generation. They are hungry for the supernatural. If they don't see His power in our lives they may settle for something counterfeit. Are you helping children learn how to live their lives through the power of the Holy Spirit?

http://kids.healthychurch.com/healthy-kids/kids-and-spirit-empowerment

Making Time for the Holy Spirit in Your Kids Service
JOSH DRYER

I love mornings. I have a pretty regular routine for my mornings. Sometimes that routine gets messed up. When that happens, there's less reading books and less enjoying the view out our bay window in the living room. However, whether my routine is messed up or not, there's always a non-negotiable to my morning: coffee. I love drinking handcrafted, freshly brewed, single origin coffee every morning. If I have to wake up early for a meeting, I make sure to wake up early enough to have my coffee.

Isn't it interesting how we make time for the things that are most important to us? If you look at your order of service for kids ministry, what's allotted the most time? What's a non-negotiable for you? Is it the skit, the fun and crazy game, or worship? All of these elements are practical, but how much time do we intentionally leave in our services for the Holy Spirit to speak to kids? Are we guilty of packing our services so tight with other elements that we don't leave margin for the Holy Spirit?

An easy way to make sure we leave space for the Holy Spirit to work is to plan with the end in mind. Instead of planning your service from the start time to the end, plan your response time first, and then work backward to the start. This allows you to think through every element and how it will direct your focus to the response time. However, the response time isn't the only time the Holy Spirit can speak to kids. Put as much creativity and planning into creating opportunities for kids to interact with the Holy Spirit as you do writing skits or designing stage sets.

"Because you have prayed" (Isaiah 37:21). These were the prophet Isaiah's words to King Hezekiah when he prayed to the Lord asking for deliverance from King Sennacherib of Assyria. After receiving a threatening message from the Assyrian king, whose army surrounded Jerusalem, King Hezekiah went to the temple, spread out the message before the Lord, and prayed. God heard his prayer and delivered Israel from King Sennacherib.

Proverbs 21:31 says, "The horse is made ready for the day of battle, but victory rests with the LORD." We can spend time planning, building, and writing, but when we spend time praying for our services and kids, God gives the victory! Praying that kids will encounter the Holy Spirit and hear from Him is one of the best ways we can spend our time during the week.

Skits, big points, and creative lessons are all ways kids learn, and they all foster spiritual growth. But nothing can maximize the spiritual growth of a child like continuous interaction with the Holy Spirit. Leaving margin for kids to encounter the Holy Spirit in our kids ministry services and classrooms must be most important to us.

http://kids.healthychurch.com/healthy-ministry/inviting-the-holy-spirit

Children and the Baptism in the Holy Spirit
DICK GRUBER

I have spent the past forty years teaching and leading children into the baptism in the Holy Spirit. If there's one thing I have learned it is that children need God's power more than ever, right now! So why wait until kids camp this year before allowing your children to enter into the fullness of God's Spirit? You can lead them into this experience today.

In Mark 1:8, John the Baptist states, "I baptize you with water, but he will baptize you with the Holy Spirit." Jesus says in Acts 1:5, "John baptized with water, but in a few days you will be baptized with the Holy Spirit." What is the baptism in the Holy Spirit? In order to help children understand and receive, let's consider what this experience is *not*. Years ago, one of my college professors shared a list of five things the Holy Spirit is not. I have expanded that to the following teaching.

The baptism in the Holy Spirit is:

- *not the same as salvation.* This is a separate and unique gift following conversion. (Acts 19:1–6)

- *not for adults only.* This empowerment is for every believer. (Acts 2:39)

- *not natural.* It's a supernatural experience. A child can't be taught how to speak in tongues. Jesus is the Baptizer. (Luke 3:16; Acts 1:4–8)

- *not just for Bible times.* This experience is for today. (Acts 2:39)

- *not an experience where tongues are optional.* Those baptized in the Spirit will receive power and a prayer language. Children take their cues from the adults around them and often pray to receive tongues. Encourage them to pray for more of God's Spirit and power. The tongues will follow. (Acts 1:8, Acts 10:44–47)

- *not a sign that you have arrived.* The baptism in the Holy Spirit is a beginning. The content of Acts occurred following Pentecost. The disciples prayed multiple times for more of God's Spirit. (Acts 2:4; Acts 4:31)

- *not scary.* God will do nothing scary to a child. I have found that once children overcome the fear of the unknown, it's easy for them to be filled to overflowing with the Spirit. (1 John 4:16–18, 2 Timothy 1:7)

When you pray with children for the baptism in the Holy Spirit:

Let them come to Jesus. Praying for the baptism should never be forced, rushed, or confusing. When children express a desire to receive the baptism, pray with them.

Listen to them. Oftentimes, children have pressing prayer requests that are more important to them than being filled with the Spirit. Listen and pray about those felt needs first. Then pray about the baptism.

Let Jesus be the Baptizer. You and I cannot baptize people of any age in God's Holy Spirit. You can't yell loud enough, shake hard enough, or hype yourself up enough to make God move in a child's life. So relax. Trust that God knows exactly when the child is ready to be baptized in the Holy Spirit. Be there to encourage and bless.

Love them. Spend time encouraging and showing love to boys and girls who have not yet experienced the baptism in the Holy Spirit. When children leave the altar after extended prayer with no apparent results, it's critical that you encourage them to continue seeking this experience until it happens (Luke 11:13).

I trust you will set aside times in children's church to teach children about, and pray for, the baptism in the Holy Spirit. Providing children with regular opportunities to enter God's presence and seek more of His Spirit are part of a healthy children's program.

http://kids.healthychurch.com/healthy-kids/the-baptism-in-the-holy-spirit

Raising Kids of the Spirit

MICHELLE WELLBORN

I am a missionary to the children in Argentina. The Lord has called me to find spiritual gold in the most difficult places—places where the natural eye wouldn't even want to go: to slums filled with open garbage dumps and horrible smells. These are the places God has called me to find His hidden treasures. My task is to find the gold, shine it, and return it to the Lord, transforming lost treasure into children of the Spirit.

After these children realize their place as heirs to the kingdom of God, and see themselves as daughters and sons of the King, we take them through a systematic basic Bible discipleship program so they understand clearly what it means to know Jesus. Then we train the children for ministry and help them understand their need to seek the empowerment of the Holy Spirit. As we lead them into spiritual empowerment, we teach them what it means to evangelize the world around them by looking for future disciples to train. Next, the children are ready to discover and develop their spiritual gifts. This is how we are creating a movement focused on reaching, equipping, and empowering the children of Argentina.

People ask me all the time why we take risks to reach, disciple, and empower children. I say behind every risk, every fear, is a testimony. My daughter was five when we itinerated a few years back, and she would run to the front of the church and ask me for the microphone. She said, "Mommy, I have a message from the Lord." I was always nervous, but I handed her the microphone and she said, "Jesus died on the cross for you, right? Because He wants you to be in heaven with Him." She is thirteen now, and she is still saying, "Mom, I have a message for the church from the Lord." What if I hadn't taken that risk? She probably would have stopped asking to give a message from the Lord.

We have seen fingers grow back, tumors disappear, arches form on flat feet, fevers disappear, swollen legs return to normal size, and the blind see. We have seen so many lives transformed by the baptism in the Holy Spirit. We are training kids to live in a culture of miracles—where living in the impossible is the norm.

If we reach and win an adult, we transform an adult. If we reach and win a teen, we may transform a family. But if we reach and win a child, we can transform a generation. There is a generation of lost, buried treasure, waiting for someone to discover them.

Children are so open to the gospel and to the supernatural. What are we doing to help them discover how God wants to use them supernaturally to build His kingdom?

http://kids.healthychurch.com/healthy-kids/raising-children-of-the-spirit

Three Things to Teach Kids About Pentecost
MARK ENTZMINGER

I want to reflect on the three primary lessons that are important for kids to learn from the celebration of Pentecost. As kids ministry leaders, here are three valuable lessons we can teach kids from the story of Pentecost:

1. *Pentecost means that the Holy Spirit no longer visits some people some of the time.* Throughout the Old Testament, we see a God who only spoke to His chosen people. Even then, He would only speak during certain times. Pentecost marks the time when that barrier was broken completely, first through the redeeming work of Christ and then through the coming of the Holy Spirit. It meant the beginning of God's promise in Joel 2:28–29 that He would pour out His Spirit on all His people. As a Christ follower, Pentecost is a celebration that He is with me all the time. It means I can know and be known by the Holy Spirit regardless of my age.

2. *Pentecost marks the beginning of the early church.* God visited the early Christians in a powerful way on Pentecost. As we see in 2 Corinthians 1:22, God put His seal of approval on that first group of people by visiting them and giving them the Holy Spirit. For kids, it's important to know that Pentecost represents the fact that church is more than a place to see friends. Instead, we gather together to celebrate God and to be involved in His great mission.

3. *Pentecost reminds us to celebrate the work God is doing and celebrate that He allows us to be part of it.* For the Jewish people, Pentecost was a celebration of the harvest. As part of the celebration, they offered to God bread baked from their harvest (Leviticus 23:17). In a similar way, Pentecost symbolizes for Christians the beginning of God's spiritual harvest in the world. For kids, Pentecost is a chance to remember that God is at work through them individually and in the lives of kids around the world. We

get the chance to be part of the spiritual harvest God is giving through the Holy Spirit.

The Holy Spirit's arrival at Pentecost can be a challenging topic to cover with kids. But when we take the time to break it down and unpack the beautiful truths from the celebration, it can be one of the most powerful stories for teaching kids about their role in God's work of reaching the world with the good news of Jesus.

http://kids.healthychurch.com/healthy-kids/three-things-to-teach-kids-about-pentecost

Ten Ways to Finish Worship Time
JOHN HAILES

It's so easy for our kids ministry worship times to become all about the singing and the dancing. We must be intentional about teaching kids the value and purpose of worship. More importantly, we must show them that worship isn't just about singing; it's about interacting with God.

We can teach kids about worship, but we need to push them out of their comfort zone to actually broaden their view of worship. Here are ten simple ways to close your worship time:

Raise and praise: As worship comes to an end, instruct all the kids and leaders to raise their hands and explain to them that we do this as a sign of praise to God. Have kids think about and speak out their praises.

Pray in groups: As worship comes to an end, instruct leaders to gather with groups of kids. Ask them to interact with each kid in the group, asking for prayer requests and encouraging various kids in the group to pray for the needs.

Spend time in silence: As worship comes to an end, ask the kids to spend a few moments in silence reflecting on God and what

He has put on their hearts. There is power in quieting ourselves before God in contemplation.

Kneel down: As worship comes to an end, have all the kids and leaders kneel. Explain that worship isn't just about singing but is about surrendering our lives to God. Remind them that this is like a servant who would bow before a king.

Pray over kids who have requests: As worship comes to an end, have kids put a hand up if they would like prayer. Ask other kids to gather around them, put their hands on their shoulders, and pray over them. Explain that we can show our love for God by loving and caring for others.

Communion: As worship comes to an end, lead kids through communion. Take the bread and juice together as you take time to remember Jesus and His sacrifice. (Be sure to clear this beforehand with your senior pastor and children's parents.)

Allow time to listen for God's voice: As worship comes to an end, provide an atmosphere for kids to concentrate on hearing God's voice. Teach kids to quiet themselves and be aware of spontaneous thoughts that God could give them. Provide Bibles, pencils, and paper for kids to read, draw, and write what they feel God might be speaking to them.

Take up an offering: As worship comes to an end, remind kids that we can continue our worship through our offering. When we give back to God from what He has given to us, we show Him how much He means to us.

Holy Spirit baptism: As worship comes to an end, invite kids to seek the baptism of the Holy Spirit. Explain Pentecost and how God wants to give boldness and power to believers through the Holy Spirit. Allow leaders and kids, who have received the baptism of the Holy Spirit, to pray over kids who are seeking this experience.

Time for journaling: As worship comes to an end, allow kids to journal (write and draw) their thoughts and feelings. Worship often creates a variety of feelings in kids that need an outlet. Journaling shows kids that worship is about interacting with God and sharing with Him what is on their hearts.

http://kids.healthychurch.com/healthy-ministry/10-ways-to-finish-worship-time

Transformed to Be World Transformers

GLORIOUS SHOO

Regardless of nationality, children across the world are learning to operate as agents of spiritual transformation. As they learn to operate through the power of the Holy Spirit, not only are they being transformed, they are also becoming transformers for those around them. God has promised to pour out His Spirit upon all flesh and this includes children.

My wife, Josephine, and I were teaching in the Bible college when the Lord spoke to us to say that we should raise Him an army. I knew exactly what He meant. So we resigned from teaching in the Bible college and started using our small rented house as a Christian boarding school. The purpose was to help orphans and needy children while raising them to be an army that would hear and follow the voice of God.

We started with fourteen children and by the end of the first year we had forty-one children in our home. Children began to learn to hear the voice of God through prayer and studying the Word of God. They would memorize a verse every day. Today we have 400 students from kindergarten through high school.

These children have been powerful in reaching out to the lost and in touching the needs of those around us. One weekend, as they prepared to minister in a hospital, a girl by the name of

Peninah from the lower elementary school prayed that she would see a miracle that day. As they prayed for the sick people in the hospital, Peninah noticed a young man, Robert, who was not able to sit by himself and could not even eat. After the group left the room, Peninah felt an urge to go back and pray for Robert. She boldly asked him to nod if he would like to receive Jesus Christ. Robert was nodding his head to show that in his heart he was repeating the sinner's prayer. In the middle of the prayer, Robert started speaking and finally could get up and eat. He walked that same day!

Another girl from a Muslim family, Ummy, asked if we could go and pray for her sick mother. A group of students and ministers went to pray. The Lord healed that Muslim mother instantly. Many Muslims in that area were prayed for and healed. Now they form a big group of believers who are part of our local church.

One evening after the normal praise, worship, and prayer in the girls' dormitory, the girls headed to bed as usual. After they were asleep, robbers tried to break into the dormitory. While the robbers were trying to push open the gate, our watchman saw a great, bright light fill the area. Then he heard people running and screaming, loud enough to wake some of the girls.

The next morning, a few men from the village met with some of our boys from the school and asked them, "What kind of powers do you use to guard your area?" They said that they were passing by the girls' dormitory when huge men, taller than our gate, jumped from inside and started chasing them until they reached the main road. We believe angels chased the men away from the girls' dormitory.

http://kids.healthychurch.com/healthy-kids/transformed-to-be-world-transformers

CHAPTER 4

outreach and evangelism

JILL DIDN'T NORMALLY invite friends to church. I don't know if that was because she was afraid they wouldn't want to go to church or if she was just shy. But this same girl filled a table with unsaved friends once a year at our annual We Love Kids event.

Joe prayed for five boys he didn't like. He wrote their names down in his Bible and prayed every day for just over four months. Then one week, he got up the nerve to tell them about Jesus. Three of the five came to know Christ. A month or two later, the others followed.

These examples of children reaching children grew out of an outreach environment. Boys and girls were trained, encouraged, and empowered to reach other children. Regular response times were the norm in children's church. Half a dozen outreach events scattered throughout the year provided opportunity and weight to the importance of outreach.

Outreach is a biblical imperative and a practical necessity for the children of our churches. If the body of Christ in your community is to grow, children and their families must come to know Christ. Apart from insuring that every class, club, and church service ends with a response time, how should a children's leader approach evangelism?

Start smart, start slow: Remember that slow and steady wins the race. Look at your church calendar and choose two to four dates when you could plan outreach events. Take on what you and your church can handle. Remember, that big church down the road has been hosting events for decades. That's why they can host six annual outreaches. Do what you can now.

Be aware of budget: Outreach events don't have to cost a lot, but they do cost something. Count the cost before embarking upon an outreach event. Make sure your church can afford to fund your vision.

Implement the pastor's vision: Be sure your lead pastor is on the same page. I served with a pastor who didn't like Halloween events. What did I do? I did nothing on Halloween! Work with your pastor and implement his vision for outreach in your community. You may have to sell your outreach idea before planning begins.

Holidays are natural times to reach out to new families: Even on a low budget, your church can add special touches to holiday Sundays. Unchurched families will be attracted to your church on Easter, Christmas, and other special days. Do what you can to help their experience as a guest encourage them to attend the church on a regular basis.

Consider this chapter to be a primer on how to reach out in your community all year long. Make the ideas your own and look for ways to encourage children and their families to reach their neighborhoods and schools for Christ. —D. G.

What Is Outreach?
AARON STRAWN

Hang on a second, I'm going to close my door and put my phone on DND (looks out the window and closes the blinds).

Ok, it's safe in here now. Let's talk about . . . outreach events. Now, I have been doing kids ministry for almost ten years and have done the Fall Fests, Christmas musicals, crusades, Easter egg hunts . . . done it all. And there's nothing wrong with those. But time and again I have found myself looking for new faces on Sunday morning . . . and . . . nothing.

What happened? Where are all the hundreds of people who were jumping on my $200-an-hour head-cracking bounce house? Where's the line of people who waited forty minutes for a snow cone? They weren't in church. Hmmm. So, should we abandon these outreach ideas altogether? I don't think that's the answer. But what is?

Well, here's an idea that might make you say, okay cool, I'll try that. One thing I have noticed about Jesus and His three years of ministry is that He never stayed in the same place very long. He didn't camp. He moved about. He went to the people, and they flocked to Him. I volunteered for two years at a local event called AppleFest. I got into the event because someone saw me do a magic act at our local library and submitted my name. AppleFest asked if I would perform, and I said sure!

I did two sets for two days. At one performance there were around 300 people. I even made the late night news! After my last performance, a family came up to me . . . Hang on, let me back up. For about a year I volunteered at our YMCA after-school program. There I met a kid named Thomas. I would play basketball with him, throw a football around, or play UNO (which I'm awesome at, btw). Ok, back to AppleFest. Up came Thomas and his mom. She said, "Thomas was so excited to see you. He misses hanging out." (The YMCA shut down the after-school program.) I then invited them to come to our Wednesday night kid's service. He showed up and never missed a week.

Here's what I learned—when I stepped outside the walls and plugged into my community, it dawned on me that this was outreach. No bounce houses, no snow cones . . . just me being there, loving on the kids of my city. Guess what—our church started to grow—I mean it exploded. So here's my point—outreach doesn't always have to be big, giant, expensive events. Sometimes, it's doing what Jesus did: going out there, loving people.

http://kids.healthychurch.com/healthy-ministry/what-is-outreach

Three Ways to Reach Unchurched Families
MARK ENTZMINGER

Barna Research recently published a new set of statistics about the unchurched in our country. Did you know that since 1990 the percentage of unchurched adults has increased from 30 percent to 43 percent of the population? Approximately 156 million people in America say they don't attend church, including more than 42 million children and teenagers.[5]

While we might not be directly responsible for reaching and discipling adults as kids ministry leaders, these statistics should still shake us. They should wake us up to the reality that there are millions of kids out there who don't live in an environment that values knowing God.

It can be challenging to figure out ways to reach unchurched families in our communities. If parents won't bring their kids to outreach events or scheduled services, how can we reach them? Let me share three practical ways you as a kids ministry leader can reach unchurched people in your community.

1. *Show them you care.* How much of our conversation and planning is about meeting the needs of the church compared with spending time and energy working to meet the needs of the families in the community who don't go to church? Ask the

Holy Spirit to show you both the needs in the homes within your community and how you might help meet those needs. When the church is family-and-community-minded you'll be amazed at how many doors will open that allow for relationships and sharing the gospel.

2. *Celebrate their children.* As you and other leaders get to know each and every child, it will be easy to take positive movement for granted. However, every parent wants to hear heartfelt and insightful truths about their child. Ask the Holy Spirit to reveal to you how He sees each child, and share those uplifting and loving thoughts with parents on a regular basis. If you don't have the time to do that on a weekly basis because of the church schedule, make a habit of picking up a phone to leave a message or sending a note through the mail.

3. *Become their friend.* I think we would be amazed at how many church leaders have not built relationships with the people who live right next to them. We can be very friendly with people who are part of the church, but to reach unchurched families we need to foster friendships with those who may never attend our churches.

Reaching unchurched families is one of our generation's biggest opportunities. We can help to change the culture one life at a time by building relationships and meeting people where they are.

http://kids.healthychurch.com/healthy-ministry/three-ways-to-reach-unchurched-families

Big Events and Follow-Up
SPENCER CLICK

Camp, VBS, kids crusades, Easter outreaches . . . all of these activities have a common factor: the preparation for them is enormous! Often the work for these big days starts nine to twelve months in advance. Big events can comprise a significant portion of your budget. Your volunteer leaders commit to the extra time needed—some even take vacation to do so.

My experience has been that ministry leaders frequently make the mistake of thinking that the last day of camp is the last day of camp or that the closing ceremony of VBS is really the end. In fact, the last day of camp is actually *the first day of the next phase for the event*—follow-up!

Follow-up helps you connect families to the church. Follow-up allows you to reinforce the experiences and lessons of VBS. Follow-up is the difference between a good experience and a great life-changing experience.

When planning an event, think of it like three sections of an orange: the buildup to the event, the event, and then the follow-up. All three are part of the process. If your event planning doesn't include a follow-up plan, then you're missing a huge opportunity to connect with those who attended and to create long-lasting impact. Was the purpose of your camp to have an experience or to create transformation? If it was simply for the experience, then don't do anything after the last day. If it was to create transformation, then the last day of camp is the time to get to work!

http://kids.healthychurch.com/healthy-leaders/big-events-and-follow-up

Leading an Invitation
DICK GRUBER

The girl knelt at an altar in Winter Park, Florida. I had just invited boys and girls to come down and pray to receive the baptism in the Holy Spirit. This twelve-year-old knelt weeping. As my wife, Darlene, and I drew near, we could hear her saying over and over again, "I'm so bad, I'm so bad."

This little girl had never set foot in a church in her life until that evening. She felt the conviction of the Holy Spirit. She knew she was a sinner. The only way she knew to express this was to say, "I'm so bad." That evening Darlene and I led her to the Lord and then into receiving the baptism in the Holy Spirit. Her case brings to mind several principles to help when giving invitations:

Let them come. Jesus said, "Let the little children come to me" (Matthew 19:14). He didn't instruct us to bribe, scare, or coerce the children to come. Let them come as the Holy Spirit convicts. Remember when giving an invitation that whether two or twenty children respond, God is the One who brings them down to the altar, not you. You can't save anybody. Salvation is a work of the Holy Spirit. Be faithful in presenting the gospel, then let children come as the Spirit draws them.

Make no assumptions. First, don't assume that children have knowledge of the Bible. Some children you encounter have never heard even the most basic Bible stories. Explain salvation in such a way that the biblically illiterate child can understand.

Second, don't assume a child is coming to the front to pray about your invitation. Most kids responding will pray about whatever you presented. Some need to pray about the pressing issues of their lives before dealing with your action point. I instruct my altar workers to ask the child what he or she came down to pray about. The child may be concerned about his grandmother. She may need healing for herself or a family member. He might want prayer for the family pet. Pray about the child's request before reintroducing the topic of your service. Once free of personal concerns, the child will easily pray about your current action point or big idea.

Third, don't assume children who don't respond are nonresponsive. Your active learners will usually be the first down to the front at every altar call. Children with other learning styles may feel more comfortable responding in their seats. Repetitive pleas due to low response only make children feel guilty or pressured. These are two motives that should be avoided at all costs.

Allow time for all children to pray. Remember, the altar only starts in the front of the room. From there, it spreads throughout a child's life. Altar time can be just as valid at their chairs as in their back yard or local mall.

Give a kind invitation. Remember back to your childhood. One day at school, you received a colorful, personalized invitation to a friend's birthday party. Two things stood out. One, it was personal. Make your invitations personal. Utilize statements like, "Some of you want to respond today," or "You are sitting there, and you know that you've sinned. Jesus loves you." Be positive in this personal approach.

The second thing that stood out about the birthday invitation is that it was friendly. It wasn't scary, intimidating, or hurtful. Keep your invitations bright, kind, loving, and calm. Quiet your voice as you present the invitation. Calmly explain, more than once if needed, exactly what children are responding to that day.

When following these simple guidelines, you will discover that children experience a genuine response to your kind invitation. Pray, work on, write, and practice invitations with as much fervor as you do the Bible story or object lesson for each week's service.

http://kids.healthychurch.com/healthy-kids/leading-an-invitation

Summer Activity Ideas
MARK ENTZMINGER

Kids look forward to the freedom that comes with summer break. Your church can take an active part in providing quality ministry experiences during the break from school. Here are just a few examples:

Summer camp: This is the granddaddy of them all! It's been said that one week of summer camp is equivalent to one year's worth of church services. While I'm not sure we can validate this statement, I do believe that no kid should miss the spiritual impact of a summer camp in a different environment. Parents and church leaders should make a commitment to do whatever necessary to ensure that no child misses camp.

Missions outreach: There is growing interest in empowering children and families to participate in mission experiences. Churches can facilitate this by setting up one-day service projects or even longer trips to a nearby community to help another church.

Vacation Bible school: Capitalize on the time kids have out of school while their parents still need to work. Provide a themed VBS outreach filled with activities kids love.

Sports camp outreach: Summer is a great time to get kids outside and active. MEGA Sports Camp provides all that leaders need to coordinate a weeklong outreach. It is similar in style to a VBS but utilizes sports themes instead. Sports and faith are great companions. MEGA Sports Camp users report a high number of visitors attending their outreach who don't come from a church background. This is a great investment in your church's summer ministry.

Backyard parties: Encourage families to get together and create events that kids will love right in their own backyards. Provide them with simple devotional content and a couple of activity ideas so you enable parents to make memories with their children and have a spiritual impact in their neighborhoods.

Whatever you do this summer, be sure to keep two things in mind. First, have a good strategy in place to ensure that every kid can participate—regardless of financial status. Second, keep your overall ministry strategy in focus and use the ideas that best fit your church.

http://kids.healthychurch.com/healthy-kids/summer-activity-ideas

Strategizing Summer Outreach

JOHN HAILES

Children's pastors today have more resources than ever to reach children who live in the shadows of the steeple. However, based on the stories I hear children's pastors tell about their summer outreaches, I get the feeling we are missing the mark by only reaching kids who are already attending another church.

There are approximately 24.6 million elementary children within the USA.[6] Certainly there are more children to reach than those who are already attending church.

Since there is no shortage of outreach resources available at the local Christian bookstore, what's missing? I'm glad you asked . . . it's strategy. Even the best outreach resource will fail at truly reaching the lost unless we answer a few strategic questions:

1. *Who do you want to reach*? If you want to do outreach, you need to know who you want to reach. Different events will attract different people. For instance, if you're interested in attracting the local Muslim population, it would be wise not to host a pig roast. Just saying!

We are located in a university town, which means a huge percentage of our parent population is drooling at the thought of their five-year-old child receiving a sports scholarship one day. So in the past we hosted a sports camp VBS and saw 350 kids attend.

Figure out who you want to reach in your community, and decide exactly where those people are located. The more specific you are about who you want to reach, the more effective you can be in reaching them. Keep in mind that to reach the people in your strategy you may need to go to them instead of trying to get them to come to you.

2. *What are their needs?* Once you identify your target, you need to get to know your target. Learn their population makeup, routines, likes, dislikes, wants, and most importantly—their needs.

The greatest outreach you can do is one that meets a need. This past summer we began a summer-long kids feeding program in an underprivileged part of town. Why? It was birthed out of a need. The local school has an extremely high percentage of kids on the free-lunch program. When summer hits, those parents still need help with their kids' lunches. Throughout the summer we fed up to sixty kids a day.

By getting to know the people you want to reach, you can strategize what you can do to reach them effectively.

3. *Who are you missing*? A good question to ask yourself in prayer is, "What are the needs of the kids in my community who are most overlooked?" Consider crafting a special outreach just for them. Find creative ways to show them the love of Jesus and to build relationships.

Sometimes I get the feeling that churches are in a bubble and are blinded to what is around them. It's also important to consider what is already being offered to families when strategizing your summer outreach.

Churches most commonly use VBS as a summer activity. While there is nothing wrong with doing VBS, we often fall into a rut of doing the same activity every year simply because it's known and is easy. I challenge you to think about the children who truly need Jesus. Where are they? This summer find ways to go to them. Throw a party in their honor, and let them see just how much Jesus loves them.

4. *What comes next?* If your outreach has been a success and children have made a profession of faith in Christ, you need to be ready for the next step—integration into your church family. Don't forget to think about what the child's/family's first service experience will be like. Will their outreach leader be there to greet them at the door? Will they need a ride? Who will go out of their way to ensure each child continues to feel welcome?

Without a strategy, you won't find your niche and you will never be truly effective at reaching the people your church is called to reach.

http://kids.healthychurch.com/healthy-ministry/strategizing-summer-outreach

Summer Outreach Assimilation
SCOTT BERKEY

As summer approaches, you are probably planning outreaches and ministry events. Summer can be very busy in the world of kid ministry, so it's important to have an attack plan before June one rolls around.

As vital as it is to plan the event, it's equally crucial to plan how you'll get all the kids to come back to church on the weekends. If your outreach event only succeeds in getting kids to come to a one-time activity, you're missing out on an opportunity to disciple kids and help them grow to become all God wants them to be.

So, how do you get kids and families to come back to your church after the outreach? Here are three keys to help you accomplish this goal:

1. *Invite them back.* As painfully obvious as this is, you would be surprised how often it's overlooked. Simply taking a few minutes during your event to let families know about your church could go a long way in helping them decide to give your church a try.

Many kids may have come with a friend or found out about your ministry event through an advertisement. They have no idea that your church offers something for them on an ongoing basis. Taking the time to invite them back for a weekend service just might be the best investment you can make.

2. *Give them a reason to come back.* If you provide kids with a reason to come back on a Sunday, can you guess what happens? That's right, they come back. A few years ago we began providing an incentive for kids and families to come back and see us after an event had ended. Usually it's something small, but at times it has been a big prize. You know your community; find a great prize to give away that everyone will love. You can even host an awards ceremony at church on the Sunday after an event. You might be shocked to see how many families come back to see their kids receive a certificate of achievement.

3. *Show them you care.* My kids love getting mail that is addressed to them. We have made it a habit to send an encouraging note to the boys and girls who have participated in our outreach events. We do this about a week to three weeks after the event has ended, and we include an invitation in the card. This is a great way to show parents that you're grateful they brought their child to your event, and it's another opportunity to encourage them to attend your church.

Make sure this summer's outreach events hit their full potential by getting kids and families to come back to church on the weekend!

http://kids.healthychurch.com/healthy-kids/outreach-assimilation

Adults Will Line Up to Volunteer for These Summer Events
MARK ENTZMINGER

Creating outreaches that kids love has never been the problem. Finding volunteers to pull off the outreaches is another story.

So what kinds of summer activities make recruiting the right workers easier? Not every activity requires a lot of manpower to plan or pull off. Tours and road trips are my favorite style of low-prep activities that both kids and adults love.

Some parents may work at places that would be cool for kids to visit. These may not tap the same volunteer base either, because approved parents who may not regularly volunteer can drive and chaperone. Here are some ideas of tours kids may enjoy:

Dairy farm
Chocolate factory
911 call center
Fire station
Old (empty) jail
Air Force base
Art studio
Print shop
Historic sites
War monuments

An easy way to help manage these kinds of events is to divide up the responsibilities in these ways:

Transportation coordinator: Make sure approved drivers have confirmed to be on site to pick up the kids and take them to the tour location.

Color-identifier coordinator: If your group is going to a public place or is fairly large, you may want to consider matching hats, lanyards, or T-shirts to help adult workers easily identify group members.

Lunch coordinator: Ask one parent to coordinate lunches for all the children and parents. This could be done by making bagged lunches in advance, or getting a deal at the local restaurant and collecting the money in advance for all the kids. By calling a restaurant ahead of time, meals can be ready when you arrive, which will reduce the amount of time to wait.

Chaperone coordinator: Recruit someone to make contact with approved parents who can accompany the children on the tour. These adults may also double as drivers or other coordinators.

Paperwork coordinator: Select one person to make sure all parental forms required by your church and/or insurance company have been received and are filled out appropriately. This person may not even need to go on the trip; they just need to be the point person to collect and verify that all necessary paperwork is completed.

Event coordinator: To make the job of the children's pastor a dream, find a team leader who will coordinate all of the logistics, team members, and promotion of the tour.

Utilizing local tours and a structure of volunteers may make this one of the most enjoyable events you do all summer. When the planning is simple and the team is strong, the leader can focus on building relationships and investing spiritually.

http://kids.healthychurch.com/healthy-ministry/summer-events-adults-will-line-up-to-volunteer-for

Five Reasons Why I Love Summer Outreach
SHEIK ALLY

Summer is my favorite season of the year. I love the weather, the schedule, and the opportunity to do something completely different in kids ministry. In the summer of 2015, we used MEGA Sports Camp as a four-day outreach that proved to be a major success. Over the course of the week, we had 70 volunteers doing everything from preparing snacks to leading small groups and we drew 140–150 kids, almost 70 percent of whom had never been to our church.

As you can probably guess, I love planning and hosting summer outreaches, and here are five reasons why:

1. *Summer outreach provides a non-threatening way for you to get to know your community.* My church is situated right next to several communities filled with families who don't spend time with us during most of the year. I don't see them on Easter or during our Fall event. But last year when I advertised our free sports camp, many of those same families participated, and a few of them eventually attended on a regular basis.

We made sure to refrain from using traditional church language in our marketing materials, and we were able to put up posters all over town.

2. *Summer outreach is a refreshing break from the norm.* During the summer, the rules are a little different. I can dress a little more casually and spend more time outside the church office. I love using the summer as an opportunity to do things with the kids that we wouldn't do during other times of the year. Water events, messy games, sports stuff—nothing is off limits as long as you can provide an atmosphere that is safe as well as fun.

3. *Summer outreach gives kids an opportunity to get out of the house.* As adults, we tend to look back on our childhood summer days with a distorted nostalgia. But for a lot of kids, summer can be pretty boring. After a few weeks of sleeping in and playing video games, they're hungry for new and exciting experiences—and their parents are desperate to get them out of the house!

A summer outreach can be exactly the kind of activity kids need to get them outdoors and active. When they're writing the inevitable "What I Did on My Summer Vacation" essay during their first week of school, they could share with their class how much fun they had at the local kids ministry outreach.

4. *Summer outreach is an opportunity to recruit, build, and train your ministry team.* Recruiting and training is an ongoing responsibility for ministry leaders. However, it can be a real challenge to bring and equip new volunteers into the ministry, en masse, during the busier times of the year. Short-term events, especially during the summer, give you the opportunity to get a large number of people involved in ministry, train them for specific positions, and evaluate whether or not they might be a good fit for your general ministry team. For volunteers, it's a chance to try out a ministry without having to make a long-term commitment.

5. *Summer outreaches are just fun!* Our MEGA Sports Camp was the most fun and most successful outreach event of our entire year of ministry. In planning the following year, it was the first event that went on the calendar.

A well-planned and well-executed summer outreach has the potential to be a huge success for you, your team, and your ministry. It gives you the opportunity to invite new families into your church and help them become lifelong followers of Jesus.

Find some resources, grab some volunteers, and make this summer the best summer of your ministry!

http://kids.healthychurch.com/healthy-leaders/summer-outreach

Three Reasons for Christmas Outreach
MARK ENTZMINGER

The Christmas season is an incredible time for children's ministry leaders to teach kids about the importance of being generous and sharing the good news with others. However, I have often wondered if there was a more effective way to teach kids how to embrace the Christmas story beyond collecting gifts on Sunday morning or Wednesday night and then distributing them through other ministries.

Stuff will never heal the hearts of children who have been born into challenging circumstances. We should give generously to these children, but not just physical gifts. We should give them our time and attention, and teach our children to do the same.

Here are three reasons why outreach should be part of your kids ministry this Christmas:

1. *It mobilizes the body of Christ.* We are called to go into the world with our joyful message of hope and joy. During this Christmas season we need to go to the poor in spirit. We can't just invite them to come to us.

2. *It glorifies the name of Christ.* We are called to know Him and make Him known. God is honored when we reach out to "the least of these." It reflects His values.

3. *It shows respect to the family and community.* It serves as a reminder that we value individuals, not just feeling good that we did something nice for someone else.

We need to teach our kids to reach out to people just as God reached out to us. He didn't give us a trinket or a toy. He gave Himself. While collecting gifts for people in need might provide a sense of temporary joy, we can do more to reach out to children who have experienced tragedy, are in the foster system, or are part of a dysfunctional family or a family going through hard times. We might teach kids that it's better to give than to receive. But even more than that, we should teach them that it's better to give themselves (their time, talents, resources, and love) rather than only giving a gift.

If Jesus were here today, would He challenge us to give a special offering or to go to people who need Him?

http://kids.healthychurch.com/healthy-ministry/christmas-outreach-and-kidmin

Five Ideas for Giving This Christmas
HEATHER MARBLE

I heard a statistic the other day that in some ways inspired me and in other ways tore at my heart: 80 percent of children don't go to church even once a month. That's a whole lot of kids who need to be reached with the love of Jesus. After hearing that number, I kept thinking and praying, "God what can we do to bridge the gap and help people get plugged into a local church? What can we do to help inspire kids to invite their friends and be missionaries in their schools?"

During my time of reflecting, I had an exciting thought—what if this Christmas season kids got excited and invited their friends to come to church? What if as parents and leaders we helped them bridge the gap! But where to start? Here are five ideas to help inspire your kids to reach their friends this Christmas season!

1. *Single parent Christmas tree*: We have so many single-parent families and parents who are just trying to get by. One way we can reach out to a family with both kids and adults joining in, is by sponsoring a family with a Christmas tree and a few Christmas presents. One of our families went out and cut down two Christmas trees, one for their home and one to give to somebody in need. The mom who received the tree broke down in tears because she wanted to give her family a great Christmas and couldn't afford a tree. It was exciting for the family who gave her the tree because they were able to create those memories and bless someone else. They also had each of their children pick out two gifts to wrap and give along with the tree.

2. *Christmas cookie invitations*: Christmas is the season of baking cookies! Last year we challenged the kids in our church to invite their friends to an Unfrozen Birthday Party for Jesus! (Living at the time in South Florida, unfrozen was definitely the way to go!)

We asked the kids to think of three friends to invite to church with them. Then they decorated a special Christmas card (glitter and stickers were a must for this project) and decorated a few cookies (frosting and sprinkles took over!). They put together a treat box with an invitation card to our Christmas Eve service. It was awesome to see the kids having fun creating and thinking about who they would invite to church!

3. *Family gingerbread decorating night:* As a family, or as multiple families in the church, people can host a gingerbread decorating night. Each person is required to bring their favorite candy to share. Throughout the night fill the room with Christmas music, snacks, hot chocolate, and laughter! During the evening you will have the chance to build relationships and reach out to the people in your neighborhood.

4. *Donate gently-used toys and clothing to a local shelter:* One family at our church does this every year. They challenge their kids during the month of December to look through all of their toys and pick out a few they no longer play with, but are still in very good condition. Then as a family they take their toys down to the local shelter and donate them to kids in need.

5. *Bless your local school:* Teachers invest so much of their own money into their classrooms. A lot of times people donate supplies at the start of the year, but by Christmas time many of those resources are used and need to be replaced. What better time to refurbish the supplies than at Christmas! Ask local teachers what supplies they would love to have replaced, and then challenge your kids to collect those items and bless the teachers. It's also a fun idea to include something personal for the teacher, like a $5 gift card to Starbucks and a small note saying something like, "Thanks a Latte for all you do during the school year. We appreciate you!"

During the Christmas season we often challenge our kids to give, but we must not forget to facilitate that challenge. These ideas will help your kids to act on the challenge. There are many other ideas as well. Be creative and know it doesn't always have to cost a lot of money to change somebody's day. One of the best ways to figure out what idea fits your family and church is to sit down and talk with your kids and see what ideas they have on ways to give back. Their creativity is amazing and you may just be blown away!

http://kids.healthychurch.com/healthy-kids/5-ideas-for-giving-this-christmas-season

Christmas Production Timeline

BRAD SHIMOMURA

Kids Christmas productions are a great way to help your children "give" during the season of celebrating Jesus' birth. This type of production is a way to get grandparents, aunts, uncles, and other relatives who don't normally attend church to come to church and hear the gospel. The key to a great presentation is excellent planning. The following is a sample timeline for planning a great kids Christmas presentation:

Summer: Search for, select, and purchase materials for the musical and/or drama presentation of your choice. Be sure to read instructions from the publisher carefully to make sure you are following all copyright requirements. Copyrights often prohibit making copies of the music CD's, so if you want to send the music home with the kids, check with the publisher before making copies.

Early September: Recruit your team. Consider having a drama coach, choir director, prop and set designer, technical coordinator, choreographer, and a few other people who can work one-on-one with kids as needed for lines, solos, or other individual needs.

Mid to late September: Introduce the music to the kids, have auditions for parts, and begin practices. Brainstorm with your team what the costumes, props, and sets are going to look like.

Early October: Cast all parts and/or solos. Finalize and begin working on set designs.

Late November: Obtain props and costumes. Have the first rehearsal with the kids on stage. Remember to practice entering and exiting the stage.

December: If necessary, have the second rehearsal, then the dress rehearsal on the weekend of the performance. Check with your sound person to make sure they receive the music in a way that is most convenient for them (CD, MP3 player, tablet etc.), and that you have enough microphones. Also, check with your pastor to see if you should present an invitation to salvation or if he would like to do that. Be sure to plan for some kind of follow-up to any who respond to the salvation invitation. Recruit a team or assign your team to restore the church stage to normal after the performance.

Day of performance: Have kids arrive early enough to do a quick run-through making sure sound, lights, props, costumes, and sets are all in order. Enjoy the performance.

Following the performance: Celebrate with the kids. Ideas include awards like "smile awards" for smiling, "energy awards" for enthusiastic performers, "attendance awards" for those who attended the most practices, and "friends and family" awards for those who brought the most guests. These awards don't have to be limited to one or two kids; you can give them out freely so everyone or nearly everyone receives an award. Most of the kids will enjoy watching the performance if it's recorded.

If the program you're considering is small, this timetable can be adjusted to fit your needs. Most importantly, schedule enough practices and rehearsals so the kids will know the songs well when it comes time for the performance.

http://kids.healthychurch.com/healthy-leaders/christmas-production-timeline

Kids Ministry and Easter Guests

MARK ENTZMINGER

Most churches spend a great deal of time, energy, and effort preparing for Easter. As children's ministry leaders, we must be careful not to miss the opportunities Easter Sunday brings our way. While it's tempting to get excited about Easter because it's one of our highest attended Sundays of the year, we must make sure to focus on each individual guest who attends.

Here are four reasons we should value important days like Easter Sunday as kids ministry leaders:

1. *Easter might be the only day a child hears about Jesus and the gospel.* We can't just gloss over Easter as simply a "high-attendance Sunday." Easter is all about sharing the gospel message so children understand what it means for them. Many children's ministries put extra effort into Easter Sunday. Make sure when adding features and elements to this special day that the message of the cross doesn't get lost. Keep Jesus in the center.

2. *Easter is one of the few days unchurched families go to church.* Forty-one percent of Americans plan on attending church on Easter, including those who regularly don't attend church. Greet these families in a way that creates a desire to return. Be creative in your interaction with new families on this special Sunday. Remember, kids will begin to frame their understanding of God based on their relationship with you and others who bear the name of Christ.

3. *Easter provides a chance to focus people around a particular vision or mission.* It's an incredible opportunity to have a large, attentive audience. What message do you want them to hear? This requires planning, intentionality, and communication. It starts with church leadership praying and listening to what the Holy Spirit might be speaking and then all working to be on the same page. Amazing things happen when adults, teenagers, and kids all work together for the same goal.

4. *Easter provides an opportunity for you to challenge kids to bring unbelieving relatives and friends to church.* What a great chance to teach about the importance of sharing the good news! Rather than enlist kids and families just to bring candy or to stuff plastic eggs, why not inspire them to invite friends from school? Or better yet, why not equip them to share the gospel before they ever get to church?

The bottom line is this: We must be intentional in creating a community where people are actively growing in their individual walks with Christ every day. If we genuinely care about reaching our communities, we must start by maximizing the opportunities we have when families and kids experience our ministry.

http://kids.healthychurch.com/healthy-ministry/kids-ministry-and-easter-guests

Presenting Easter in Context
CHRIS CORBETT

Has anyone ever told you a story completely out of context or started a story in the middle rather than the beginning? Both can be frustrating. What often happens in either of these cases is the original meaning of the story gets distorted or minimized.

As we think about teaching the Easter story, we need to consider how to present the accounts in such a way that kids understand they aren't a series of isolated events. The Easter account is the climax of the biblical narrative. It's a part of a story that started many years ago. When we teach "Jesus is alive" on Easter morning, we are communicating the fulfillment of prophecies that happened years before.

Here are a few things to keep in mind:

God has been working out His plan for humanity's redemption since the beginning of time. Connecting the death and resurrection of Jesus to the creation narrative gives kids an understanding that the events of Easter have been a part of God's plan since sin entered the world.

Emphasize the Bible as one story with a central theme. A theme of the Old Testament is that Jesus is coming—it sets the stage for the events in the New Testament. We can't fully understand the significance of Jesus' ministry, death, and resurrection without understanding the problem of sin presented in the Old Testament.

Remember that God is the main character of the Bible. He reveals Himself to us through the person of Jesus. The Easter account is about God making a way for humanity to be reunited with Him.

Show kids how the ministry, birth, death, and resurrection are prophesied in the Old Testament. For example:

Isaiah 7:14 and Matthew 1:23 (Jesus will be called "Immanuel")

Isaiah 53:12 and Matthew 27:38 (Jesus will be crucified with criminals.)

http://kids.healthychurch.com/healthy-kids/the-climax-of-the-biblical-narrative

How to Connect with Easter Visitors

MARK ENTZMINGER

It takes intentional effort to draw first-time guests—whether kids or parents—into our ministry. Really making an impact and ensuring that guests don't simply show up annually on Easter takes preparation and foresight. We need to be proactive rather than reactive about our Easter Sunday visitors.

Here are just a few ways you can intentionally connect when you welcome guests on Easter Sunday:

1. *See the church through their eyes.* This one is hard, because it's easy for us to overlook a stack of paper or poor signage in the parking lot or church entrance. But it's critical! To help you understand how your church is viewed by newcomers, consider going to an unfamiliar church as if you were an attendee and see what you notice. Or ask some new attendees what their biggest challenges were when they started attending your church.

2. *Greet the children first.* Nothing speaks of your values to a parent more than making sure you notice and engage their children in conversation. Rule #1—Slow down! If you're frantic on Sunday mornings, you won't have the time to connect with parents who are visiting. Rule #2—Look kids in the eye! You may need to get down on one knee to do this, but it makes connecting much richer. Rule #3—Learn kids' names. If you want parents to know you love their kids, use their child's name in a positive statement when they come to pick up that child—without needing to look at the child's nametag.

3. *Speak life.* Even when you aren't conversing with a new guest they'll be listening to your tone, body language, and words. Don't get caught being negative and condescending.

4. *Instruct regular attendees about their responsibility to welcome guests.* Life at church takes on a different tone when everyone is seeking to greet and befriend new guests.

5. *Instruct regular attendees how to make the environment open to the moving of the Holy Spirit.* If you want new guests and nonbelievers to know how to respond to the Holy Spirit, then all of

your church members should model this throughout the service. When your regular attendees are taking notes, opening their Bibles, worshipping, praying, etc., this says to a new guest, "We believe this is important and real." This will help guests be willing to respond to the leading of the Holy Spirit.

6. *Provide important information to the parents before they ask.* Good signage and concise information about your church is crucial. You must look at this through the lens of someone who has never been before and may be cautious about coming to church. How easy is it for guests to find times, locations, phone numbers, and information on your website? What kind of print resources are available that explain how to know Jesus? Do you have printed resources that describe all the church activities people can get involved in? In what ways do you help parents understand your check-in system and make sure they're comfortable with it? How do you handle a parent who isn't comfortable leaving their child with people they don't know in an unfamiliar environment?

7. *Listen.* God gave you two ears and one mouth. Maybe this was for a reason.

I want to encourage you to be intentional when you meet and follow up with families who are visiting your kids ministry at Easter. I think kids and parents alike can tell the difference between being greeted because they are another warm body in the room and being greeted because volunteers and leaders are genuinely glad they have visited and want to get to know them.

http://kids.healthychurch.com/healthy-ministry/connect-with-easter-visitors

CHAPTER 5
kids and grief

HER NAME WAS Alice. She was eleven years old on that Saturday morning. Her dad and another man from church were hit head-on by a drunk driver while on their way to a church softball game. Alice's father survived, the other dad didn't. With tears in her voice, Alice told me that her friend Julie's dad was dead. Alice's dad was in a local hospital with a few broken ribs. Thus began a journey of walking alongside Julie's family and our children's church as all grieved the loss of this father.

My first three years in children's ministry found me walking through death, divorce, and other tragedies with kids and their parents. I have to admit that when I began as a children's pastor, I only saw the fun side of this ministry. I dreamed of great children's services, exciting outreach events, and joyful club meetings. Experiencing the painful side of ministry never entered my young mind.

Children and their families will experience loss. The death of family members, friends, and even favorite pets can devastate a child. Divorce, injury, or the trauma of school bullying can affect a child for months or even years. I have learned a few rules of thumb for assisting children with loss and grief.

Be there—in every church setting. I have provided children with my phone number. They are told each week that they can call me any time. Loss doesn't typically occur between 9:00 and noon on Sunday. Children need to know you are accessible when they need counsel or prayer.

Don't try to fix things. It's important to listen to, hug, pray for, and support children and their families through hard times. You don't need to provide answers or solutions. Sometimes a quiet friend is what a family needs more than a biblical exposé on pain.

Think long-term. Most churches are pretty good at helping a child or family through the initial stages of grief, but it's important to continue to befriend and assist a family for months, or even years following a loss.

Everybody needs a listening ear when facing fear and loss. You provide a steady Christ-like influence throughout the ordeal. Allow children to express their fear, anger, and questions without jumping to conclusions or making quick judgments.

This chapter contains a collection of blogs dealing with this darker side of children's ministry. The writers have provided insight and practical answers to some tough issues. The words that follow will help you personally and assist you in your response to tragedy in families or the church body. —D. G.

Helping Children Navigate Trauma
MELISSA SUNDWALL

There are a few guaranties in this life. One of them happens to be pain. It's not a subject we like to dwell on because pain isn't something we look forward to. Occasionally we use the adage, "no pain no gain." When we recite those words we are implying there's something good at the end of the pain. And while that's true in some scenarios, how do we live with pain that seems to have no gain? When our world is shaken by disaster, or our life is forever changed by a traumatic occurrence, we desperately need the care and presence of friends and family and a deep connection to our Savior.

As leaders in the church, if you haven't already walked with a child in the midst of pain, you will. Adults have a difficult time making sense of pain. Just imagine one of the children in your ministry living with pain that makes no sense to him. I would like to offer suggestions to help you minister to kids in pain.

1. When we help a child navigate a loss or trauma, we need to be tuned in to the fact that they may come to some illogical conclusions. For example, the child has experienced some sort of disaster. They may internalize, "I'm not safe." In this example we need to do more than tell the child he is safe. He routinely needs the physical experience of safety.

2. Listen for "I" messages that indicate how the child really feels and the conclusions he is coming to about himself and the world he lives in. Children naturally focus on the part they play in an event or story, which means they often over emphasize their role in traumatic events. For example, when children go through the divorce of their parents it is very common for them to believe that somehow it was their fault or their actions contributed to the divorce. These "I" statements could sound like, "It's my fault" or "I'm bad."

3. Be present. Kids need to have an adult example that helps to make God real to them in the moment, whether they're sad, angry, or frustrated (1 John 4:11–12 NLT). There are examples in the Bible of people expressing their feelings e.g. Martha—grief (John 11:20–27 NLT), Jesus'—anger (Matt. 21:12–13 NLT), David—confusion (Ps. 22 NLT). God isn't offended by our feelings. In fact, being honest with God is an important step in the healing process.

4. As you minister to children experiencing pain, keep Jesus' words in mind, "What is the price of two sparrows—one copper

coin? But not a single sparrow can fall to the ground without your Father knowing it" (Matt. 10:29 NLT). He is faithful to us in our times of need. As we walk with kids through times of sorrow, pain, or trauma, we can know that God will answer their call. He will be present with them. King David reminds us, "Even when the way goes through Death Valley, I'm not afraid when you walk at my side. Your trusty shepherd's crook makes me feel secure" (Ps. 23:4 MSG).

http://kids.healthychurch.com/healthy-ministry/helping-a-child-navigate-trauma

How Parents Can Help a Grieving Child

KEITH SWARTZENDRUBER

My earliest memory of grief was the diagnosis of my mom with breast cancer. I was five years old. All that I knew at the time was the overwhelming feeling of being shaken and challenged. I felt a combination of emotions—loss, fear, doubt, confusion, and instability. Those emotions came to a climax with the loss of my mom at the age of fourteen.

Throughout my family's battle with my mother's illness and death, I recognized that my parents and family coped the best they possibly could. They sought to help me manage the mourning process properly. However, my experience with grief at a young age has helped me realize that parents and adults are often at a loss when helping children navigate through the grieving process.

Below I have listed three basic ways to help parents be better prepared to help young children deal with loss.

1. *The truth is always the best.* Many times well-meaning adults and parents cause added damage to the grief process by not telling the truth. Children don't think abstractly. They can only use concrete thinking to reason. Telling a child that Jesus took Grandma

up to the sky may cause the child to look for Grandma on the rooftop. Or the child may wonder if Grandma is in an airplane that flies overhead. A youngster may feel anger against Jesus for taking Grandma away. Give your child basic simple truths that help them understand. For example, "Grandma's body stopped working and she is now in heaven. Heaven is a great place to be."

2. *Include the child.* Oftentimes our first response is to shield children by not including them in the grieving process. This can cause children to feel unimportant and can hinder their healing. Instead, give them an option to participate in the funeral. If they do choose to participate, prepare them for what they may experience.

3. *Help your child deal with emotions.* Times of loss cause a wide variety of emotions. A child's emotional development is often incapable of managing these feelings. As mature adults, we must prepare ourselves to help them process these emotions. Start by being patient in answering all of their questions. Use stories or fables to help a child understand the difficult emotions. Allow time to process and remain supportive.

During times of loss, it's important to reassure your child constantly of the hope we have in God. The hope that we can spend eternity with God and our loved ones reassures your child of God's goodness and grace. These simple truths will help support your child while navigating through grief and loss. Such truths will last a lifetime.

http://kids.healthychurch.com/healthy-leaders/help-for-a-child-navigating-grief

The Holidays and Grief
AARON SCHAUT

I'll never forget that night. As my two young boys excitedly hung ornaments on our Christmas tree with Grandma and

Grandpa and holiday music played in the background, I sat on the couch fighting back tears. I was trying to keep that night the great family tradition it had always been. I struggled to control my emotions, but it was too much for me. I crumpled onto the couch and let the weeping take over. *Amy is supposed to be here*, I thought. *This is her thing!* It just wasn't the same without her.

For most of us, Christmas is a time of joy, filled with warm memories of friends and family—as it should be. But for those who have lost a loved one, the holiday gatherings and celebrations can be challenging. Having lost my wife a month before the holiday season ten years ago, I would like to share a few ideas from my experiences of how we can help others who are dealing with loss in their lives.

Allow for the grieving process. Each person's grief is different. Allow them the freedom and dignity to express their hurt and healing process in their own way. Don't tell them how they should feel. The people who helped me the most were the ones who felt comfortable with (or at least allowed for) my expression of emotion, and sometimes lack thereof.

Just be present for them. Grief is never clean, easy, or predictable. Ministering to people who are dealing with loss is messy, and that scares people! No one likes being in a situation where they don't know what to say—or worse yet, where they might say the wrong thing. The natural response is to avoid such situations, which means avoiding the person who has experienced loss. But for a person in grief, it's not really about what you say; it's about simply being there. Those who God used most in my healing process were those who weren't afraid to be around me and just be themselves. I'm so thankful to the people who loved me enough to risk being around me. They chose to invite me into their lives and didn't alienate me because of my situation.

Give them the opportunity to be "normal" again. Invite those who are grieving to engage in everyday life activities with you. Give them the opportunity to feel normal again and to have permission to go through holiday traditions with you. Those who have lost loved ones need to experience that while life will be different, that doesn't mean it has to be bad.

Understand that God is the ultimate healer. Only God can heal a broken heart. In fact, Scripture tells us that He is close to the broken hearted. "The LORD is close to the brokenhearted and saves those who are crushed in spirit" (Ps. 34:18). Trust that God will provide the strength and peace that is needed for the grieving process. And be thankful that God is using you to bring healing in another person's life.

http://kids.healthychurch.com/healthy-ministry/the-holidays-and-grief

A Child's Spiritual Development and Divorce
KEITH SWARTZENDRUBER

Family ministry in the church today focuses on the responsibility of the parent as the primary discipler of their children. The role of the church is to support parents in this endeavor. Blended families have additional challenges as they disciple their children. Often children in divorced families face a two-headed monster. In other words, they have two of everything—two families, two houses, even two sets of rules and guidelines. Their faith and church life is no exception. The child may observe various acts of worship and doctrinal differences based on what church or churches they attend. The child may question if they should stand or sit to sing. Should they make a cross with their hands or fold their hands for prayer? And the ultimate question, "What must I do to get to heaven?"

Here are some helpful ideas to tame this two-headed monster:

1. *Parents must be intentional in establishing faith in their children.* The child's spiritual development should not be overlooked by the challenging circumstances of family life.

2. *Parents should do their best to answer the "whys" regarding a child's faith.* Helping a child to understand the "whys" gives them a clear understanding as to what it means to be a follower of Christ.

3. *The church should plan activities in order to accommodate children living in divorced families.* Giving them every opportunity to participate helps to build and strengthen their connection within the church body.

4. *The church can offer strong role models who can help fill in the gaps for single-parent households.*

5. *The church can help bridge the gap between Sundays and holiday seasons when a child must be absent.* It's important to give children from blended families and single-parent households the opportunity to access lesson material online or by other means. This allows the child to stay connected even when they must be absent.

6. *Church leaders can give clear instructions on how and why we worship the way we do.*

Children are vulnerable to the negative effects of divorce. It's important that parents and the church partner together, ensuring that families of divorce keep their focus and priority on the child's spiritual development.

http://kids.healthychurch.com/healthy-leaders/divorce-and-discipleship

The Church: A Long-Term Partner

MARK ENTZMINGER

First Corinthians 3:6 hints at the long-term approach the church should have as it relates to ministry. Paul planted the seed, Apollos watered, and God is the one who makes it grow.

Our world is in desperate need for a long-term partner. Most organizations treat helping others as if they are on a conveyor belt in an assembly line. They reach the church, the church evaluates their situation and provides them with a solution . . . and is done with them. However, the church was never designed to function that way. When we see people in need, it's critical that we slow down and become the church that Jesus died for—a church that will do whatever it takes to bring people to salvation.

I want to share some of the needs in our society for which the church can be a solution. It will not likely be mutually beneficial, but it may just snatch people from the flames of judgment (Jude 1:23).

Divorce care: Our society treats divorce as a norm. However, there's nothing normal in the life of a child who is living through the tearing apart of the family. As families blend together, a whole new series of challenges arise.

Poverty and homelessness: Don't let the stories of those who abuse the system keep you from finding a way to provide long-term assistance to those who are deep in poverty or are homeless. (Find a homeless shelter near you: http://www.homelessshelterdirectory.org/)

Foster care and adoption: There are nearly 450,000 children in the foster system on any given day in the United States. These kids need the love of godly homes. The families who take them in need support and encouragement. Families who are adopting encounter unique challenges and adjustments. (thechurchisthesolution.com, compactfamilyservices.org)

Abused and neglected children: There are so many forms of abuse and neglect of children in our world today. Consider just this one ministry, Project Ignite Light (ignitelight.org), which provides important personal items to children who need to be examined at Children's Advocacy Centers around the U.S.

Immigrants: There are political answers for the situation we face with immigrants in the U. S., but before we are members of a political party, we are members of God's church. He calls us to love our neighbor as ourselves, and extend clothing, covering, food, and care to those in need. Our neighbor may not speak the same language we do or even practice the same religion, but our commitment is to love them as Jesus does.

Special needs: Churches are waking up to ministry with children who have special needs. However, there's still more to be done. Ministry to these families should go beyond Sunday morning to provide support throughout the week as well. (myhealthychurch. com/specialneeds)

The ministry of the church isn't a conveyor belt on an assembly line. It's a journey of human beings who love and care for other human beings in the name of Jesus Christ.

http://kids.healthychurch.com/healthy-ministry/the-church-a-long-term-partner

Helping Children Find Hope in Difficult Times
MELISSA SUNDWALL

One of the most challenging things we do as children's leaders is walk with our kids or team members in times of pain or disappointment in life. For many of us, our first inclination is to make the pain go away and help the person get their life back to normal as quickly as possible. I think we often respond this way because we don't like to see people suffer, especially a child. Another reason may be our own discomfort. Walking with people through these times can be uncomfortable, and they can last longer than we anticipated. We find the place of prolonged ambiguity that often accompanies times of pain and disappointment uncomfortable.

I would like us to consider times of ambiguity, disappointment, struggle, or loss as opportunities for our kids to experience God's care and His personal interest in their lives. As we come alongside children or adults during difficult seasons of life, how can we best minister to them so they feel supported within a community of caring Christians?

Stay in the journey with them. Most church communities respond well to the practical needs that surround a disaster or traumatic event. They provide things like food, water, clothing, hospital visits, transportation, etc. But when the initial event blows over, all that is left is the pain. What many people experience is that once the practical work is done, the support presence disappears. It's so important that kids feel the presence of God's community not only caring for their physical needs but also their emotional needs. During these times we have the opportunity to model God's continued, caring presence to the child. When children experience this, trust grows. They learn that God is with them in good times and in difficult times.

Don't feel like you need to provide answers to all their "why" questions. It isn't our job to answer all their questions. The most loving thing we can do for either an adult or child in crisis is to help them connect with God in their pain. The Holy Spirit will provide the "God" answers they need. He will speak to the heart issues. Ask the Holy Spirit to help you facilitate this process.

Help the child have their own experience with God. During these times of ministry to kids, they need more than lectures on behavioral issues or information about what God can do. They need to experience Him for themselves. Help the child get in touch with God. Use music, or allow them to express themselves to Him through art. Perhaps they need to vent their anger to Him, or allow the sadness to spill over through tears. As we make room for the child's emotions and invite God into the moment, we communicate to the child that God cares about them individually and that it is good to communicate their feelings to Him.

Though the pain and suffering of life is never considered enjoyable, it's often in those times that new treasures are discovered in our journey with God. He can redeem the unwelcomed trials of life to teach us that as we reach toward Him, our hands will never come back empty. "The LORD is close to the brokenhearted; he rescues those whose spirits are crushed (Ps. 34:18 NLT).

http://kids.healthychurch.com/healthy-kids/finding-hope-in-difficult-times

Can You Recognize the Hurting?

MELISSA ALFARO

Are there any poor among you? Many times we relate "poverty" with the lack of financial resources, but according to educator Dr. Ruby K. Payne, poverty is defined by "the extent to which an individual does without resources"—a void of the financial, emotional, mental, spiritual, physical, relational/role model, support systems.[7]

As long as we are encountering people, we will come across the "poor in spirit." Perhaps it will be our students in ministry, colleagues, fellow church members, or other people who cross our paths in life.

They may hide behind their ministry, their work, or even materialism.

They may isolate themselves, pushing away from pivotal relationships in their lives.

They may disconnect—releasing responsibilities and detaching themselves from their church family.

They may expose their discouragement through their demeanor and talk.

Or . . . they may mask it well.

But one common thread is . . . they are hurting. There is a missing "peace" in their lives. Too many times we spend our days trying to diagnose the pain of someone rather than just being there for them. Regardless of what hurt they are experiencing, as believers, we are equipped to be expressions of God's love and care here on this earth. How do we do that?

How do you recognize the hurting and be with them?

1. *Be aware.* Take notice of individuals you haven't seen in a while or changes or transitions taking place in their lives or families. Be intentional about reaching out to them.

2. *Be present.* Love is spelled T-I-M-E. Many times the hurting aren't crying out for something but for the presence of someone. Be available and ready to listen.

3. *Be authentic.* Don't resort to cliche statements or try to identify the perfect solution for their problem. Just stay close as they navigate through the process.

4. *Be generous.* If it's within your power to do so, be willing to meet their physical needs. If you have a tangible resource that they are lacking (food, clothing, etc.), be willing to give that resource as an expression of God's love.

5. *Be sensitive to the Holy Spirit.* The Holy Spirit will teach you how to pray for them, how to love them, and give them hope in Jesus. Follow His lead.

A healthy disciple is not only aware of the hurting but is also willing to simply "be there" and walk through the healing process with them.

http://kids.healthychurch.com/healthy-kids/recognizing-the-hurting

CHAPTER 6

volunteers

RELUCTANTLY, JOHN BEGAN helping in children's church to assist his wife, who had excitedly volunteered to be part of our team. He told me at the first team meeting that he was only there because of her. He said, "I'm not an up-front guy. I won't do anything up front in this children's church for at least six months." So I put the date on my calendar. Six months later I put John up front, and he liked it. Today, that more-than-reluctant volunteer is a children's pastor.

The search for volunteers in children's ministry is never ending. Just when you get enough helpers to fill every spot, somebody leaves. Or better yet, your ministry grows. Although many children's leaders dread the hunt for the perfect volunteer, some have learned to embrace, and yes, even enjoy this aspect of children's ministry. Here are some keys to enjoying the adventure of the volunteer hunt.

Recruit for the future. When is enough, enough? *Never!*

Make recruiting a spiritual act. Encourage the prospective worker to pray about committing to this ministry.

Don't recruit teachers. The T word tends to scare the average Christian. Instead, recruit role takers and snack helpers and craft assistants.

Pray about it. Jesus exhorts us to pray that the Lord of the harvest will send laborers into the harvest field. Pray about your volunteer needs every day. Prayer still works!

Provide continued care and support for those already in service. When word gets out that your department takes care of its leaders, your volunteer force will begin to grow. Be a blessing and you will in turn, be blessed.

This chapter is dedicated to the great volunteer hunt. Many of those reading this portion of the book may feel that this chapter alone makes it worth the retail purchase price. The ideas presented here will revolutionize your volunteers and your approach to this critical aspect of ministry to children. —D. G.

Is Your Kid's Ministry Fueled by Coffee?

JOSH DRYER

Nowadays, everyone (okay, not everyone, but most) starts their day off with a cup of the sacred bean in some form. Drip coffee from the Mr. Coffee pot at home, an overheated latte from Starbucks, or some frozen concoction blended with a lot of sugar and a hint of coffee. Coffee "fuels" many of us and helps get the day started right! I want to ask this question: Is your kids ministry fueled by coffee? Below is an acronym that will help you find out.

C—Celebrating Wins

Nothing puts a jolt of energy into your kid's ministry team like celebrating wins! When your leaders have clearly defined objectives and then celebrate when the team achieves those objectives, that sparks something inside the team and drives them to win more!

O—Outreach Oriented

The great commission is to reach the lost. In his book titled *If*, Mark Batterson says, "We're called to advance the kingdom, not hold the fort." Our kids ministry should be fueled by reaching those kids in our community and city who have never heard the gospel message, not by having the latest and greatest technology or the funniest puppet sketch!

F—Fostering Friendships

One of the missions of our church is "to be a church that experiences community." We're driven to connect people with a faith community. When kids are surrounded by other kids who are seeking Christ, they're fueled to keep going and encouraged along the way. Also, they foster friendships that will last a lifetime and will help them make positive choices rather than negative ones.

F—Family Focused

The family is one of the most important biblical statutes under attack by the Enemy. If the Enemy destroys a family, he's not taking down just one person, but the whole tribe. We need to fuel parents and families with resources that will help them play offense rather than defense!

E—Encouraging

Hopefully kids in your ministry aren't drinking coffee (or that will fuel them for all kinds of craziness)! Encouraging a kid or leader by the power of words will fuel them to dream higher and achieve more. First Thessalonians 5:11 says, "Encourage one another and build each other up." A kids ministry fueled by encouragement does just that: it builds world changers!

E—Equipping

There are few things in kids ministry more important than allowing kids to encounter the Holy Spirit. When you build in time for kids to hear the still, small voice of the Spirit, they are fueled and challenged far more by Him than by anything you could say or do. Allow the Holy Spirit to be the equipping fuel to the image-bearers of God who sit in your kids ministry.

http://kids.healthychurch.com/healthy-ministry/is-your-kids-ministry-fueled-by-coffee

Four Functions of a Safety Team

MARK ENTZMINGER

I think I can hear you say already, "Are you kidding me, Mark? I can barely keep my rooms staffed, and now you want me to have a safety team?"

That's right. A safety team can provide a different level of benefit to your children's ministry that most teachers and volunteers are too busy to spot. Although you may have a hard time finding leaders for a classroom, having positions on a security team may help people "get their feet wet" in children's ministry while providing a key service to your church.

Consider the following functions of a security team that would benefit every church:

Watching for unusual behaviors: This isn't to imply they're watching for kids who are acting up. As a safety team they can observe the kids to see if anyone is bullying, if there is a suspicious adult hanging around the area, or if an activity may get a little dangerous. The security team is visible and should be easily identifiable as being involved in keeping the kids safe (consider a vest, name tag, or lanyard). Parents also like to know there are people assigned just to watch for the safety of their kids.

Creating safety plans: There's a lot to think about when considering the safety of kids: evacuations, allergies, medical situations, people who intend harm, kids who go missing, etc. Rather than trying to develop plans and train leaders about their appropriate responses for any potential need, assign this responsibility to the security team. Then review their work. Once your church leadership agrees on the plan, set up times for them to train your volunteers about the responsibilities of the safety team and how they will interact with other volunteers.

Calling for medical assistance: With an appropriately staffed safety

94

team, you can have people equipped to know when to call 911, and/or an on-site medical professional who is willing to assist in case of emergencies. This safety team could all be trained in first aid and could help prevent well-intentioned, but medically untrained, leaders from making costly mistakes if someone is injured or becomes sick.

Extra eyes and hands: I don't recommend that a safety team be utilized as ministry volunteers as this would distract them from their focus on safety. (If they want to be involved in ministry, by all means replace them on the safety team and move them into ministry.) However, they can be an extra set of eyes and hands to make sure that when a child heads to the restroom no one goes in after him or her. They can be equipped to watch for "escape artists" and be trained to know how to bring them back to the group. By having a safety team who covers these functions, it will help the ministry volunteers stay focused on ministry.

It's no secret that there's a lot of administration involved in children's ministry, and adding one more piece may seem like a significant undertaking. But when you take the time to invest in various teams, you will see your leadership ability expand. By having a safety team, you allow other leaders and volunteers to focus on relational ministry with the children.

http://kids.healthychurch.com/healthy-ministry/four-functions-of-a-safety-team

Encourage Your Volunteers
JESSICA DOWNS

You have done it. You finally have all the volunteers you had been hoping and praying for. But you begin to notice them slip away as fast as you gain them. What's going on? You try to make sure they have all the materials they need and even have helpers in their class. What more could they possibly want?

One word: *encouragement.*

Generally speaking, it's easy to be on the receiving end of encouragement, but it can be a challenge to give encouragement. What do you say? And how do you say it? What if your team member really didn't do anything deserving of a "well done"? I'm here to tell you that everyone needs positive words spoken over them even if they don't earn it.

I know it seems counter intuitive, but if all you ever do is correct your volunteers (or say nothing at all), they won't last long. We all have insecurities, and unless someone speaks directly in opposition to them, they can get the best of us. Imagine if your senior pastor only spoke correction over you. Seriously, think about it. How long would you stay in your position?

Most of our volunteers don't have formal training, so from the outset they probably have lots of uncertainties about their ability to work with kids. But when we come alongside them and encourage them in their journey, it gives them the strength to keep growing and moving forward. So how do you do that? Here are some suggestions:

Verbal encouragement: Make a point to say something to each volunteer you see on the weekend. Whether it's a "Looking sharp this morning!" or a "Thank you for your faithfulness each week!" Don't underestimate the power of a positive word.

Written encouragement: Consider writing three to four thank-you cards each week. Keep track of who you send them to so you don't miss anyone. This does two things: It encourages your team, and helps you look for things that went well instead of just the things that went wrong.

Spiritual encouragement: Intercede for your volunteers. Find out what they need prayer for and go to bat for them in the spiritual realm. Include verses or devotionals in your team communications and let them know that you pray their relationship with God is deepened through their service.

Physical encouragement: Show up for your team. Invite them into your home. Attend your teen helper's high school play. Offer to babysit for a couple in your ministry. If you're invested in them, they'll be invested in you.

So there you have it: four ideas for supporting and encouraging your volunteers. You may not be able to implement all of them right away, but start with one and add more as you are able. Bit by bit you'll see the difference a little encouragement can make.

http://kids.healthychurch.com/healthy-ministry/encourage-those-that-volunteer

Growing with Your Team
BRENT COLBY

I wanted our church to have lasers. My friend's church had lasers, and it seemed to make all the difference to his kids ministry. They had remodeled their children's ministry wing, and it was loaded with the latest gadgets and amenities. Slides? Check. Touch screens? Check. Lasers? Check mate. I convinced my pastor that I should visit the church to see what the lasers, I mean church, looked like in action. I drove over on a Wednesday and was blown away by what I saw; but it had nothing to do with lasers and everything to do with a healthy, growing ministry team.

This made me realize that the health of my ministry had nothing to do with lighting. The health of my ministry was determined by the individual health of my volunteers. While the environment that my friend had created was cool, it paled in comparison to the friendly, prepared, and engaging leaders he had stationed throughout the church. I realized that the secret sauce to his ministry had nothing to do with facilities but everything to do with his growing team.

We often fall short when it comes to the development of ministry volunteers. Let's be honest: It's easier for us to spend time organizing supplies or building sets. But the greatest return on investment you could ever make is always an investment in people. Understand this: *Thriving ministries are characterized by leaders who grow with their teams.*

It all starts with leaders who grow. If you want your team to grow, then you must be committed to your own growth. How intentional are you about personal development? Do you set goals, assess your own strengths and weaknesses, or ask experienced ministers for advice? There are many ways you can grow as a leader. It's important that you initiate some type of learning experience that meets a current need or goal.

Growth becomes contagious when you share it with others. That's right! Don't keep all the ideas to yourself! Find ways to bring other people into your growth experience. Host training events, pass out books, and dedicate time to explore new ideas. There are countless ways to foster an environment of growth with your team. Be purposeful with your team-time, and don't neglect to share teaching moments with others. This critical step of bringing others on board doesn't need to be complicated—but it does need to be intentional.

The ministry at the "laser church" wasn't successful because of their cool facilities. It was successful because of their ability to learn and grow as a team. Healthy leaders know this and connect personal growth to the growth of their team. Lasers are still awesome, just less awesome than the possibility that you can begin to grow with your team today.

http://kids.healthychurch.com/healthy-ministry/growing-with-your-team

Three Keys to Adding More Volunteers to Your Ministry Team

BRIAN DOLLAR

It's a question people ask me on a regular basis: "How do you get folks in the church to volunteer when they think it's the job of the children's pastor to do the ministry?"

This is one of the most difficult tasks of a kids ministry leader—recruiting volunteers. I can tell you, there's no secret formula. The only way to recruit successfully is through continuous hard work and adherence to a few key principles. Here are three important keys that I have found helpful:

1. *Don't recruit from a need; rather, recruit from an opportunity.* There's nothing worse than a children's ministry director standing up in front of the congregation and saying, "We are so overwhelmed. We must have help. Please help us!" That tells the person listening, "There must be a reason no one is working with them."

Never say, "No one wants to help" or "I can't get anyone to help me." That's like my son starting off a question, "I know you are going to say no, but . . ."

Rather than moan about how much you need help, choose to celebrate the growth and excitement of your kids ministry. Don't talk about what you *don't* have, talk about what you *do* have—opportunities for the members of your church to make an eternal impact on souls for whom Christ died.

2. *Recruit from the vision of your ministry.* Start by raising the value of children's ministry inside your church. Share stories in church services about life change in children or have volunteers share stories about how their lives have been changed. Serving in children's ministry is an opportunity to honor God—not a duty or a task (Col. 3:23).

Recruit by giving people an opportunity to be a part of what God is doing in the lives of the children of your church. Explain, "God is going to accomplish His plan in the lives of the children in our church. The question is not 'Will God do it?' The question is 'Will you be part of it?'"

3. *Recruit one-on-one and face-to-face.* Rather than use a blurb in the bulletin, a video announcement, or a pulpit spot from your senior pastor, recruit by approaching people one-on-one and having a meaningful conversation with them.

Ask God who He is preparing for service (Luke 10:22). Once He leads you to someone, approach that person. Don't just walk up in the hallway at church—that doesn't communicate to someone that you value them. Instead invite them to lunch, call them on the phone, or go out to eat with them after church.

Explain to them that as a result of what God is doing in your children's ministry, an opportunity has arisen. You have been praying about who the person should be to serve in this area. You felt led to talk to them because you feel that they have the right gift mix to make a difference in the lives of these kids for the kingdom.

I know that adding volunteers to your team is a lot of work, but I can honestly tell you that every bit of that work is worth it! Get out there and build your team so you can win the lost!

http://kids.healthychurch.com/healthy-ministry/3-keys-to-adding-more-volunteers-to-your-miniistry-team

Trained Volunteers Are Effective Volunteers
MARK ENTZMINGER

There are some topics in children's ministry that are commonly practiced. These would include how to discipline, how to communicate with specific ages, etc. But I want to encourage you to consider some training topics that may not be a normal part of your process:

Safety: How frequently do you cover safety training with your leaders so they know what to do in the event of inclement weather, fire, or unauthorized persons engaging with kids? Consider having the Red Cross train teachers in basic first-aid practices.

Reflective listening: Training people how to use curriculum and teach age-appropriate content is common. However, the art of listening and reflecting back to the class (more importantly, the speaker) what was communicated is a skill that can reap large benefits.

Gender differences: I have seen churches provide training on the different age-appropriate levels of learning as well as give understanding of learning styles. However, gender also plays a significant role in helping kids receive what is taught. Each gender has a unique preference in how they learn and respond to content. If we aren't intentional in training our leaders, we may unknowingly frustrate the learning of boys or girls. To see an example of this training, download our document on *Capturing the Hearts of Boys and Girls*.

Why we do what we do: It's one thing to teach people how to present an object lesson or a game that reinforces the verse, but don't miss the importance of sharing the why behind the what. Replicating an activity without knowing the why can lead to mission drift and weakened effectiveness.

Injuries: It's only a matter of time before someone gets a skinned knee, there's an instance of biting, or possibly something worse. Knowing the first-aid process approved by your church leadership and insurance company is essential. This must also be something that is trained to the leaders within the ministry.

Special situations: There will always be things that happen outside our control and training. Be sure to acknowledge these times as a reality that leaders will face, but give them a framework for what to do. Equip them to know who they should notify, how to complete the appropriate safety report, how to respond to parents, etc.

Training is an ongoing process, and there will always be new topics to communicate. Keep a list of elements for staff training, and begin to gather resources to provide that training. Once the resources are developed, you can easily pass them along to a new leader.

http://kids.healthychurch.com/healthy-ministry/training-topics-not-to-miss

Give Volunteers a Break
GAY WALL

Volunteers are one of the most valuable resources within any organization. This is true whether it's the local church, the district office, or the national office. They are people who care and choose to serve beyond their normal responsibilities. Since volunteers are a gift from God and the engine that moves ministries forward, leaders need to honor their service by intentionally protecting them from burnout.

Leaders who give volunteers a good written plan during recruitment build trust, confidence, and relief that they are not entering an open-ended commitment. People work with more energy when they know that the ministry respects their time and wellbeing.

James Robbins, an organizational leadership trainer, says, "Over the years I have worked with hundreds and hundreds of volunteers. They are awesome. As much as volunteers are amazing, finding them has never been more challenging. People are busier now than they have ever been in history. This shortage has meant that many volunteers are taking on more than they can handle, resulting in volunteer burnout. Burnout at the volunteer level is a very serious problem and in fact, when a volunteer overextends themselves for too long, the consequences can be huge.... In fact, when volunteers quit because of burnout, it takes a long time to get them back. So when you think of the volunteers that you lead, remember, if you don't take care of them and help manage their load, you might end up losing them for a very long time, if not for good."[8]

I want to repeat that last sentence, "So when you think of the volunteers that you lead, remember, if you don't take care of them and help manage their load, you might end up losing them for a very long time, if not for good." Careless leadership can do short- and long-term harm to God's gift of volunteers by not managing their wellbeing.

Here are a few resources to help us develop a good volunteer plan that will lessen the chances for burnout:

Kelly Anton describes *10 Ways to Prevent Volunteer Burnout* from her personal experience as a volunteer mom in PTO, sports, and Scouts. These tips are equally relevant to the church world, where many parents are volunteering with their children at school and at church. James Robbins provides a few additional suggestions in his 5 *Steps for Preventing Volunteer Burnout*.

How to Prevent Volunteer Burnout challenges us to take care of volunteers using a quote from Elizabeth Andrew as a cornerstone: "Volunteers do not necessarily have the time; they just have the heart."

Heather Joslyn and Christine Yackel give pointed insight in their article, "How Charities Prepare Volunteers for Intensely Emotional Work." This seems particularly valuable to service ministry volunteerism, as we know that the work with children can often be emotional, which adds another layer of consideration in selecting, caring for, and keeping volunteers.

My top four takeaways from these resources are:

Have a personal connection with your volunteers—let them know they're more than just filling a role or need in your ministry. "My heart is . . . with the willing volunteers among the people" (Judges 5:9).

Have clear communication and a clear understanding of what each volunteer is supposed to do. Communicate with reminders, thoughts, and/or praise about what the volunteers are doing and give updates as needed.

Continually give appreciation, praise, and thanks to your volunteers for their commitment, dedication, and service. Give more than just at Christmas time; give thanks often throughout the year. "When the people willingly offer themselves—praise the LORD" (Judges 5:2).

Plan time off periodically. Volunteers may not want to disappoint you, but they still need a break. It's best if you can already have time off scheduled in your volunteer guidelines.

http://kids.healthychurch.com/healthy-ministry/give-volunteers-a-break

Developing Volunteers with Limited Time
ADAM LAWLEY

"Can't make it!"

"I'm too busy this week, work has been crazy!"

"Sorry, I have a previous engagement."

These are a few of the dreaded phrases we have all heard when it comes to volunteer training. In a culture that seems to get busier and busier each day, time is precious. A. W. Tozer once said, "When you kill time, remember that it has no resurrection." Time isn't something we can get back; we must treat it like a commodity.

This presents a dilemma for ministry leaders, "How can we prepare our volunteers who have limited and precious time?" We simply can't bypass training and hope they figure it out. Strong volunteer teams are the backbone of a successful children's ministry. Let me share some ways to prepare busy volunteers:

Meet them where they are: A possible solution to the dilemma is to meet our volunteers where they can be met. Today, more than ever, we can connect through a variety of options, e.g. Facebook, Instagram, YouTube, Face Time, video chats, and other social media. We have the ability to utilize these platforms to their fullest potential. Meeting our volunteers where they are allows us to develop leaders in a busy world. When utilizing these tools for training, remember that every second counts, so try to be concise and fun!

YouTube: Instead of having a bi-monthly meeting, send out bi-monthly videos of training content. This format allows your material to be scripted and carefully prepared. This may seem daunting, but the process can begin with a simple push of a button on a smart phone.

Video chat: Rather than a one-on-one meeting prior to a church service, have a video chat with a volunteer during the week. In these video chats you have the ability to be personal, as well as to receive live questions.

Customize it: You know what works best for your volunteers. Training can take place with volunteers through e-mail, volunteer-specific social media profiles, or even a private Facebook group. Have fun and make it your own! Allow your vision to spread beyond Sunday mornings.

Celebrate wins: Take time to encourage your team; mention all that is successful. Include a story or testimony of what God is doing in the lives of the children.

Appreciation: Let them know how treasured they are to the church's ministry. Thank them!

Be practical: Provide training that's memorable and applicable. Discuss policies, conversation starters, or potential ministry opportunities.

Challenge: As the leader of the ministry, you are able to cast the vision. Take advantage of this time, challenge the volunteers to take ownership of the ministry and the vision.

http://kids.healthychurch.com/healthy-leaders/developing-volunteers-with-limited-time

Communicating with Your Team

GAY WALL

Communication—good or bad—affects the atmosphere and environment of your ministry. It can determine your ability to keep a great team together. In church work, where a leader is more dependent on volunteers than in most organizations, the need for great communication is even more critical.

Someone said, "It's not what you say, but how you say it," but I believe it should say, "It's how you say what you need to say." When you communicate well with those you lead, it helps eliminate confusion and encourages an exciting, healthy, and peaceful ministry environment. Recruiting volunteers is easier in this kind of atmosphere.

Here are a few ways to help you communicate better with your teams and volunteers:

1. *Meetings*—Yes, meetings! I know we all have too many meetings, but it's easier to communicate our passion and feelings to our teams in an open meeting. In a meeting, they not only hear what we are saying but experience the feelings connected with it.

2. *E-mails, Facebook, texts, Instagram, and tweets, oh my!*—Yes, in this day of multiple ways to communicate, we should use them all. It enables us to pass messages to our teams without disrupting their busy days.

3. *Add a dash of humor.*—It's okay to laugh while you are being serious! If we can show confidence and seriousness with some humor, we can captivate our team, lower any tension, and create an effective atmosphere. Just make sure the humor is appropriately communicated. Sometimes it's harder to see humor in a text.

4. *Can you hear me now?*—Speak plainly and share clearly what you want others to do or know. It's good to write the key points of what you want to communicate on a whiteboard and ask if what you wrote is what your audience understood. If there is some misunderstanding, then reframe what was said so everyone can be on the same page.

5. *Keep it pleasantly simple and use body language.*—We want to show that we are passionate about what we are communicating. No, we don't have to dance, but we can show excitement! A change in our delivery tone can amazingly redefine the words we are using.

6. *I can hear you; can you hear me?*—Yes, listening is part of communicating. Let's encourage our teams to share their thoughts and be open about disagreements. Listen to what your team has to say and consider all they share. Feedback helps us measure how we are communicating.

7. *Practice a little one-on-one.*—Sometimes a team member may need one-on-one attention. Our time is limited, so this one is more sacrificial, but we don't want to leave any team member behind.

8. *Express thanks often.*—Thankful and appreciative leaders affirm their teams and let them know that their time, energy, and

work are important. Showing appreciation is crucial in keeping team members from burnout.

http://kids.healthychurch.com/healthy-ministry/communicating-with-your-team

Recruiting Kids Ministry Volunteers

MARK ENTZMINGER

A vibrant kids ministry requires passionate people who are inspired by a vision and are well-equipped to live it out. But how can you ignite that passion in your church as a way to recruit new volunteers to serve in your ministry?

I want to share some creative ideas to help you overcome the challenge of getting people plugged into ministry.

Provide a "test-drive" opportunity that allows people to try out serving in kids ministry. Set aside four to six Sundays a year when you give people the opportunity to find out what it's like to serve as a kids ministry volunteer. This shows people that you're more committed to helping them find the right opportunity to serve rather than using them to fill an opening. This is an excellent way to get volunteers plugged into any type of ministry, and it's incredibly effective at providing church members with an "inside look" at your children's ministry.

Work with other staff members to find creative ways to help people find their place in the ministry your church is doing. This is a great idea I found after reading a post from Joshua Kansiewicz. Essentially, the staff at his church takes the time to identify potential volunteers who aren't serving, and invites them to a connections event. Those attending the meeting share what they have learned about their passions, personality, and strengths. The pastoral team assesses their understanding and response to the gospel, answers any questions they have, and helps them get connected to the right ministry. Working with your team to create an event like this is an incredible way to solve the volunteer challenges across your entire church. A simpler approach is to invite church members to a "volunteer fair" type of opportunity that highlights the various areas of ministry and allows them to choose one that resonates with them most.

Stop doing everything yourself and start building a team. Something probably needs to stop so you can begin investing in people and inviting them to join your team. The leader who pours into students can't minister to every student. The leader who loves kids can't personally invest in every kid. We need to equip others to multiply our influence. When you take the time to build a team rather than being involved in every aspect of ministry, you can focus more on recruiting volunteers and solving other ministry problems.

I'm not proposing three easy shortcuts to double the number of volunteers you have overnight. However, these strategies can help you recruit and retain volunteers in the long run. If you're interested, here's a great starting place for kids ministry leaders who want to build a team of volunteers and a culture of ownership within their ministry.

http://kids.healthychurch.com/healthy-ministry/recruiting-kidmin-volunteers

The Dilemma of Teen Helpers
RACHEL PILCHER

I first helped in my church's kids ministry at age fourteen. I began by helping with basic crowd control and ended up teaching a three-year old Rainbows class. My call to ministry started while I was serving as a young teen in the kids ministry. I believe I became a kids pastor because I grew up in a church that allowed and equipped me to serve.

So how can you involve teens in your kids ministry? We all know you can't just let teenagers loose in your ministry and expect success. It takes time, training, prayer, and more training! It might require more effort to have teens involved in your ministry, but in so many other ways it makes your ministry better! Yes, it's a dilemma, but imagine a kids ministry once you begin using teens as volunteers.

1. *Teens bring high energy to your ministry.* They are loud, boisterous, and love to have fun! They can get away with things that you would never dream of because they're young. Teens create a fun environment for your kids!!

2. *Teens are role models.* Whether you like it or not, your kids look up to them. So use teens for good. You can mentor, train, and disciple them. Let their "immature" behavior rub off on your kids!

3. *Teens are willing to do what adults can't or won't.* Many of us have regularly walked into classrooms and witnessed adults standing in a corner visiting with each other (that's a different blog!). Teens, on the other hand, love to play dress up, sing silly songs, and comfort a child who is nervous about staying. Teens may be young, but most are willing to do whatever you ask them to do.

4. *Teens are teachable, where adults often are not.* Teens are still learning and desire to do their best. They want their leaders and pastors to be pleased with them. Pastors can speak into their lives easier than into the life of an adult, who may not be as teachable or as open to instruction.

How can you include teens into your kids ministry?

1. *Chat with your church's leadership.* It's important to have their guidance and support in any new ministry endeavor.

2. *Create a list of available areas where you can use teens in your ministry.* (Examples: greeters, check-in, sound, media, worship

team, preschool helpers, small group leaders, etc.) Always start new teens with these options and as you see growth, leadership qualities, and a teachable attitude, begin to give them more responsibilities.

3. *Create a teen volunteer commitment form.* Since you are working with teens, you'll need to provide a clear outline of expectations and responsibilities for them and their parents. Require parents or a guardian to sign the teen commitment form. If parents are aware of the commitment of their teen, then they'll be able to help encourage and get them there! Make sure to write and include a discipline policy for your teen volunteers. Finally, I also recommend having them complete these forms at the beginning of each school year.

4. *Regularly provide training and discipleship.* Working with teens requires more training and discipleship than working with adult volunteers. You'll have to provide correction and discipline with your teen volunteers at some point. The more you disciple your teens, the less you'll have to correct them.

5. *Let them lead!* Once you have a great start for your teens, step back and let them lead. See their potential and allow them to flourish in ministry. Let them fail! Remember the best lessons are learned from our failures.

Two years ago I was looking for someone to take over the praise and worship of our kids church services. I reached out to my lead pastor, and he gave me a list of names to contact. I began to pray over the names and reached out to them. One by one they turned me down. I was frustrated. I prayed again for God to help with a solution. That same week we went to kids camp. The worship team was a group of teens from a different church in our district. Several teens from our church went as helpers and staff. They spent the week watching and worshipping with the teen worship team. Teens from my church spent time in the altars praying and worshipping with our kids (motions and all). God provided the answer! Our teens caught the vision and our praise and worship time was never the same!

Why not capitalize on teen talent and desire? There's no dilemma for me in working with teens. I won't work in a kids ministry that doesn't utilize teens and their serving hands!

http://kids.healthychurch.com/healthy-ministry/the-dilemma-of-teen-helpers

Getting People Plugged in to Ministry
MARK ENTZMINGER

Recruiting volunteers who have a true passion for discipling children is one of the most difficult challenges you face as a kids ministry leader. At the same time, you might feel like there's not much you can do without owning the process for getting people plugged into ministry.

As a children's pastor, you might not be able to formulate your church's assimilation process, but there are definitely things you can do to speak into it. Here are three ways you can play an active role in your church's connection process and recruit volunteers who are passionate about kids ministry.

Equip your connections team with resources beyond information about open volunteer opportunities. One of the easiest ways to get people excited about volunteering in kids ministry is to make it exciting. It sounds obvious, but this is something we often forget. Rather than simply letting your connections team know about the volunteer positions you need filled, what if you created resources they could share that highlight all the incredible things going on in your ministry? It could be something as simple as a few testimonies from kids in your ministry or an engaging video that highlights all the various ways to get involved.

Train your current volunteers to actively recruit new volunteers. You'll never have a volunteer problem if you train volunteers to constantly look for others to serve. What if you had to worry about finding roles for volunteers to fill rather than finding people for roles? That's what happens when you create a culture of multiplication where volunteers understand the importance of being involved in ministry and are actively recruiting others to serve. For example, what if you challenged your volunteers to recruit one person every six months who's not volunteering in another capacity, to serve in your children's ministry? By the end of the year, you could possible quadruple the number of volunteers in your children's ministry.

Develop a process to learn more about the people in your church. Can the characteristics you are looking for in a volunteer be discovered through conversation, personality assessment, or other methods? If so, develop an intentional process for gathering this information at events or other connection points. It could be something as simple as observing church members on Sunday to watch where they might be naturally gifted. Another opportunity is to work with your pastoral team to create a survey that asks people about the areas of ministry they are interested in.

A healthy, growing kids ministry will always have new opportunities for service—and it will always need new volunteers. As a kids ministry leader, the best way to support your church is to equip your connections team and volunteers with tools that help them steward people through the process and help them get plugged into the volunteer role that's right for them.

http://kids.healthychurch.com/healthy-ministry/getting-people-plugged-into-ministry

Recognizing the Signs and Symptoms of Untrained Volunteers

DICK GRUBER

In four decades of ministry to children, I have been blessed to serve alongside some of the best volunteers on this planet. While serving with volunteers and being a volunteer myself, I have discovered two truths. First, volunteers long for care. Second, volunteers will not reach their full potential without training. Let's leave volunteer care for another blog and focus on signs and symptoms that your volunteers aren't receiving enough training.

The untrained volunteer believes he is serving his time in the children's department. He arrives just seconds before class time and can hardly wait to leave when it's over. He complains to everybody but his leader. He is grumpy, unprepared, and unpleasant. His portion of the class time is disorganized, confusing, and lacks creativity. Burnout is his battle cry and bitterness his breakfast.

Right now you may be thinking, *I know this guy. How do I get rid of him and find a winner?* I propose to you that he is that winner! Jim Wideman writes, "Maybe your next superstar helper has already been recruited–but you haven't coached star-level performance out of that person yet. Look for potential in people and work with them."[9] With a lot of love, and a training plan, a sad excuse for a children's leader can become your next superstar.

How does that happen? First, pray. Seek God's wisdom on behalf of this leader. Next, spend time with that leader. You have to learn to like him first. Look beyond his current performance and discover his future strengths.

Let me address the characteristics described above:

"Serving his time" syndrome—instill a passion for his involvement as service for the King and not just a job.

Tardiness and immediate escape—inspire a love for the children that extends beyond the classroom and time. This is described by Paul in 1 Thessalonians 2:8.

Complaining spirit—encourage a spirit of gratitude in the volunteer. You may also need to teach appropriate conflict resolution skills.

Grumpy—involve him in creating an atmosphere of godly joy in your children's department. It's hard to stay grumpy when you're working to help those around you become joyful.

Unprepared, disorganized, or lacking creativity—invest in time management and lesson-design training for this person. Teach a variety of storytelling and Scripture teaching methods to all workers.

Burnout and bitterness—insure that this volunteer, and all your volunteers, experience regular Sabbath times. God didn't design anyone to serve constantly for years without a break.

In the book *The Disney Way* the authors write, "Train extensively and constantly reinforce the company's culture."[10] As a leader of children's leaders, you must implement a culture of constant training and support for volunteers. Well-trained volunteers who know you have their backs will serve in a positive way for extended periods of time.

Here are a few basic tips for training:

- Training is more caught than taught. Most volunteers easily implement what is modeled for them by a competent teacher.

- Training begins with a passion for children's ministry. This passion, or vision, will motivate people to serve even under the worst conditions.

- Training includes a plan to produce the highest quality fruit in the lives of children.

- Training is about building the people, not the ministry.

- Training places emphasis on *who* a volunteer is more than on *what* they can do.

http://kids.healthychurch.com/healthy-ministry/untrained-volunteers

notes

1. https://www.zerotothree.org/early-learning/brain-development
2. http://www.livescience.com/25908-newborns-learn-native-language.html
3. T. Berry Brazelton, *Touchpoints 3 to 6: Your Child's Emotional and Behavioral Development* (Boston: De Capo Press, 2002).
4. http://www.pewforum.org/2016/03/22/the-gender-gap-in-religion-around-the-world/
5. https://www.barna.com/research/state-church-2016/
6. www.childstats.gov/americaschildren/tables/pop1.asp
7. Ruby K. Payne, *Framework for Understanding Poverty: A Cognitive Approach* (Highlands, TX: aha! Process, Inc., 2012).
8. James Robbins, *Nine Minutes on Monday: The Quick and Easy Way to Go From Manager to Leader* (Columbus, OH: McGraw Hill Education, 2012).
9. Jim Wideman, *Children's Ministry Leadership* (Loveland, CO: Group Publishing, 2003), 103.
10. Bill Capodagli and Lynn Jackson, *The Disney Way* (New York, NY: McGraw-Hill Books., 2007), 10.

list of contributors

MELISSA J. ALFARO, PhD, girls ministries director, Texas-Louisiana Hispanic District, Houston, TX; founded a gender-specific mentoring leadership program for ESL and at-risk middle school students in the public school system and received two grants (2007-2010), author of *The Day the Princess Cried: The Diaries of the Biblical Princess of Lamentations 8*; FB Melissa J. Alfaro ; Instagram pastor_melissa

SHEIK MOZART ALLY, kids and family pastor, Calvary, Orlando, FL; founder of ilovekidschurch.com; @sheikmozart

SCOTT BERKEY, executive pastor, Victory Worship Center, Tucson, AZ; national director of children's ministry for the General Council of the Assemblies of God, 2011–2013; conference/camp speaker; @scottberkey/twitter

DAVID BOYD, national director of BGMC for the General Council of the Assemblies of God, Springfield, MO; https://www.faccbook.com/david.boyd.12979

RANDY CHRISTENSEN, children's and family pastor, Hillside Church, Mankato, MN; former president of the World Clown Association; www.qualityprograms.net; follow Randy on Facebook at Randy Christensen and twitter at pastorclown

SPENCER CLICK, senior pastor, Calvary Lighthouse, Lakewood, NJ; http://twitter.com/spencerclick/ https://www.facebook.com/spencer.click

BRENT COLBY, children's ministry director, Northwest Ministry Network, Seattle, WA; brentcolby.com

CHRIS CORBETT, DMin, professor, Southeastern University, Lakeland, FL: Chris Corbett (Facebook)

BRIAN DOLLAR, associate pastor/kids ministry, First Assembly of God, North Little Rock, AR; creator of High Voltage Kids Ministry Resources, author of *I Blew It!* and *Talk Now and Later*; facebook.com/brian.dollar @briandollar1 briandollar.com (blog)

JESSICA DOWNS, children's pastor, Eastridge Church, Issaquah, WA, MrsDowns11 (FB, Insta, Twitter)

JOSH DRYER, kids pastor, First Assembly of God, Fairbanks, AK; https://www.facebook.com/JoshSDryer

MARK ENTZMINGER, senior director of children's ministries, General Council of the Assemblies of God, Springfield, MO; https://www.facebook.com/markentzminger

CINDY GRANTHAM; https://www.facebook.com/cindy.grantham.58

DICK GRUBER, DMin, professor of children and family ministries, University of Valley Forge, Limerick, PA; https://www.facebook.com/dick.gruber?fref=ts

JOHN HAILES, next-generation pastor, Urbana, IL; https://www.facebook.com/jhailes

ADAM LAWLEY, middle school pastor, Victory Church, Lakeland, FL; https://www.facebook.com/aclawley

HEATHER MARBLE, children's pastor, Life Church, Roscoe, IL; Facebook.com/hjmarble

DAN METTEER, associate pastor, Creekside Church, Lynnwood, WA; adjunct professor of children's ministry, Northwest University; co-author of *Fusion Children's Ministry* series; Facebook.com/danmetteer, Twitter @danmetteer

RACHEL PILCHER, kids pastor, Victory Life Church; FB: https://www.facebook.com/rachel.l.pilcher; Instagram: rachelcpilcher

CARA RAILEY, gender ministries consultant, General Council of the Assemblies of God, Springfield, MO; @cararailey

AARON SCHAUT, administrative pastor, Central Church, Green Bay, WI; FB Aaron Schaut; Twitter @aaronschaut

BRAD SHIMOMURA, missionary, Assemblies of God World Missions, Japan; find Brad on facebook, twitter and instragram: shims2japan.

GLORIOUS SHOO, president, New Life Foundation, Moshi, Tanzania; https://www.facebook.com/glorious.shoo

AARON STRAWN, go-kids pastor, River Valley Church, Farmington, MN; https://www.facebook.com/aastrwn

MELISSA SUNDWALL, licensed counselor, owner of Sundwall Counseling and Beyond Studio, Springfield, MO

KEITH SWARTZENDRUBER; https://www.facebook.com/keith.swartzendruber.7

GAY WALL, children's ministry director, Georgia District of the Assemblies of God; https://www.facebook.com/gay.wall.9

MICHELLE WELLBORN, missionary, Assemblies of God World Missions, Buenos Aires, Argentina; https://www.facebook.com/mtwellborn

JIM WIDEMAN, children's ministry pioneer, author, speaker, and coach, Nashville, TN; @jimwidemanT, I facebook.com/jimwidemanministries; jimwideman.com

for more information

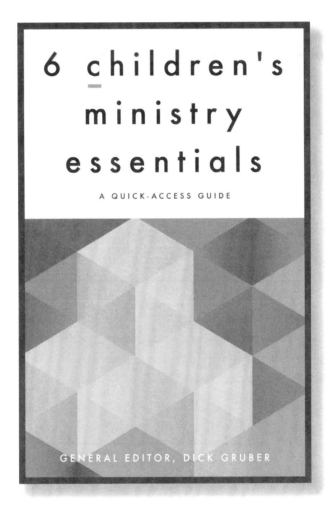

FOR MORE INFORMATION about this and other valuable resources, visit www.myhealthychurch.com.